THE ESCAPE ARTIST

Matt Seaton was born in Brighton in 1965. He has written for numerous newspapers and magazines, and is currently a contributing editor to *Esquire* and the parents editor of the *Guardian*. He coedited and contributed to Ruth Picardie's *Before I Say Goodbye* (Penguin, 1998). He is married and lives in London with his two children.

For more information on Matt Seaton visit
www.4thestate.com/mattseaton

THE ESCAPE ARTIST

Life from the Saddle

Matt Seaton

FOURTH ESTATE • *London* and *New York*

This paperback edition first published in 2003
First published in Great Britain in 2002 by
Fourth Estate
A Division of HarperCollins*Publishers*
77–85 Fulham Palace Road
London W6 8JB
www.4thestate.com

4

A catalogue record for this book is available from the British Library

ISBN 1-84115-104-1

Typeset by Palimpsest Book Production Limited,
Polmont, Stirlingshire
Printed in Great Britain by
Clays Ltd, St Ives plc

In memory of Charlie Curthoys, 1962–2002

Prologue

*I was not yet sixteen when I understood a great deal,
from having ridden bicycles for so long, about style, speed,
grace, purpose, value, form, integrity, health, humor, music,
breathing, and finally and perhaps best of all the relationship
between the beginning and the end.*

— William Saroyan

There is a point as you reach Westerham Hill from the north
side where the gradient finally levels off. Despite the chill air,
you are sweating hard from the exertion of the last twenty
minutes' ride up the steady incline. At Keston church, perched
bravely on the side of the hill, the walled graveyard almost
slipping down the slope with the advancing years, you join
the A233 from Bromley. Your legs are heavy then and hurting
from the short fierce climb up to the main road. You leave the
bike in a small gear for a few extra seconds as you go over the
top, to spin the burn away while your pulse levels off and you
catch your breath again.

From there, the A233 rolls towards the final southernmost
ridge of the North Downs. The route dips occasionally with
the contours, but in the main makes a slow, steady ascent of
the escarpment. In summer, when your muscles are warm and
work better, the long drag is flat enough to force you to push

a big gear. In the winter, in the off-season, you would use the small ring, turning a smaller gear to save your knees and keep the tempo brisk. Only with a cold north-easterly at your back, blowing you along, or after the turn of the year when you are beginning to think of 'the pipe-openers', the early season races, only then might you slip the chain on to the big ring and remind your protesting legs what hard-earned speed feels like once again. So you learn to measure the passing of seasons by the selection of gear ratios. The quick glance down between your legs is to check which cog the chain is wound on, wrapped in its snug mechanical embrace. But the North Downs are not the Alps, and on this road a middle gear is fine.

The A233 is one of those ancient roads that leads into the countryside towards nowhere in particular. It must once have been a droveway for the sheep that were herded down from the Weald and over the North Downs to market. No modern engineer would have built a road that plunges so steeply down from the ridge into the village of Westerham. As it drops, the road bisects the Pilgrim's Way, and near Keston it passes an old Roman mausoleum and a site known as Caesar's Camp.

It is only ten minutes since you left the last housing estate of West Wickham, once a village and still a Kent postcode, though now sewn seamlessly into London's southern reaches. Another few minutes takes you to the old RAF station of Biggin Hill, its gradually decaying brick and concrete compound commanding a flat saddle of downland. The Spitfire and Hurricane that guard the entrance sit in their chocks, permanently grounded.

Through the village of Biggin Hill itself, the A233 bears left and heads south. As you toil up the drag, you pass through the last patches of woodland which suddenly opens on to a vista of variegated green, brown and grey. On a winter's day, under the diffused light of a low flat sky, the countryside's colours are a dirty camouflage. At Westerham Hill you have reached the final ridge of the North Downs. On either side the hills form a great rampart, stretching away into the hazy distance to where the land falls away vertiginously to a deep, wide valley. Tucked out of sight, sheltering below in the southern lee of the Downs, lies the Pilgrims' Way. The medieval lane jogs around the patchwork fields and hedgerows, passing half-forgotten churches and chapels, on its way to Canterbury the other side of the M25 motorway.

On the far side of the old A25 rises the Weald of Kent. Mist hangs over what remains of the once great forest. Remote and unkempt by comparison with the chequered fields of the neatly tilled lowlands, the Weald still bears the promise of an English arcadia unsullied by cars, roads and the suburban overspill of London.

You have just time to sit up and take in this view. You might take a second or two to straighten your back, stretching to banish that grumbling muscular ache below your kidneys. You take your hands off the bars to zip your thermal jersey right to the neck, cruising for a moment in the manner of stage-winners in the Tour who straighten their jersey and adjust their cap so the sponsors get their money's worth when the cameras start clicking. Then, as your freewheeling gathers pace, you are back on the North Downs on a winter's day and your gloved hands quickly seek the bars. This time, rather than rest on the tops, they grasp the drops, two fingers delicately brushing the brake levers in readiness. Touching, but with no pressure: you want the speed. The speed is the reward for the effort of riding up here.

The road now falls away sharply under tree cover. There is no need to pedal; the bike accelerates rapidly past the point where pedalling would be effective. You move into a tuck, making your body as small as you can into the wind, spreading your weight as low and evenly as possible over the bike. In the autumn, your eyes would be scanning the road for wet leaves, that can form a skein of slime as treacherous as ice. But the winter's rains have washed the surface of detritus. Still you watch for potholes and stones.

You are in free-fall. You are aware of nothing but the line you need to take. A few minutes before, the sound of your labouring lungs was your constant companion. Now, in the background there is just the roar of the wind and the pulsing of blood in your ears.

The road makes a hard bend to the right and then straightens to point directly downhill to the valley floor. If the surface is dry and you are running on good tyres, if the way is clear of traffic and you can use the width of the road, if you have all your courage and wits about you, you can make it round that curve without touching the brakes. You hit forty-five, fifty, right at the apex. You cannot see the exit and it is crucial to pick the right line. If you start running out of road, the camber will be against you, shrugging you off the blacktop. Once committed to a line, it is too late to use the brakes. To crash at this speed is unthinkable.

And then, in a split second, you are round and free. You are still upright, and the road stretches out in front of you again. You cannot believe your luck, you are alive and intact. You feel the chill of the air as the wind slices through layers of clothing, greedily sucking away the body's heat from damp undergarments and the scorching tears on your cheeks. But the cold does not hurt. You have taken flight.

Descending demands skill and courage and a lack of imagination. To imagine too much is to wake up in the middle of the night sweating, jerked awake by the thought of what might happen if you fall. The Italian racer Gianni Bugno, twice world champion in the late 1980s, once joked that when his confidence was at its lowest he had become so fearful of descending that he would ride down mountains like a priest in a cassock. To descend like that, with your hands grabbing the brakes all the way, unable to believe that the next hairpin can be negotiated at more than walking pace, is not an option for the professional cyclist. Bugno's cure was to listen to Mozart on headphones as he rode down the mountain. The music blocked his fear, soothed his brain and allowed him to trust in his reflexes. With the *Magic Flute* he learnt to fly once more.

A certain willed stupidity is useful to the cyclist – the type I was, a racing cyclist. To train as hard as you must merely to be able to race, to reach the minimum standard of fitness and speed and stamina necessary even to finish a race, let alone to win a *place* in one, for that you need to acquire this willed stupidity. The racing cyclist must be a Nietzschean hero without an idea in his head. The goal, attainable by slow degrees, is to be fitter and faster, to be able to push on beyond those moments when the body is begging for respite. To race well, you have to be willing to make whatever sacrifice is necessary to transcend yourself, again and again. You have to push yourself and it has to hurt. You have to put out of your mind the burning desire to stop by the side of the road and take a rest. For the racing cyclist, there is always another hill, another sprint, another lap, another mile. The dogged belief in your own perfectibility works like a drug; it makes you feel chosen to belong to an elite.

However hard you think you ride when you train, nothing can replicate what actual racing asks of you. At first, when it hurts too much, you quit the race, you *pack*. But in time you learn that it is possible to ride on sheer willpower alone. *Dig in*, they say to you, and you discover that you have reserves of strength you never imagined. You *hang in*. You discover that you hurt less if you can make others hurt more, so you mount an attack. You feed off their pain: their weakness makes you stronger. At the height of his powers, Eddie Merckx – arguably the greatest, most aggressive racer that ever lived – was known in the peloton as The Cannibal.

For the racing cyclist the key objective is to slip the bunch, to mount an attack and ride away from the main group. Sometimes this will be in company, making temporary allies of other racers; sometimes it will be solo. To attack, though, you must be confident that you can ride faster than the bunch. So, to shake off the peloton, you must be confident in your ability to ride through the pain and sustain the escape. The bicycle race has a natural narrative trajectory – a beginning, a middle and an end – and the escape is a plot device, a delicate matter of tactical judgement, timing and psychology. But mainly you must be willing to suffer. I have seen friends finish races with slumped shoulders and eyes unfocused like a shell-shocked soldier's. And I have seen myself reflected in their blank exhaustion.

At the beginning of his *Big Adventure*, Pee-wee Herman has a dream of winning the Tour de France. Over the line he speeds on his beloved red bicycle, still wearing his suit and bow tie, to the acclaim of the crowds lining the avenue and the despair of the other professional racers. This affectionate pastiche of a bicycle-obsessed fetishist contains a kernel of truth, for everyone who has mounted a racing bike has dreamt of riding down the Champs-Elysées at the *tête de la course*. The bike-racer shares a portion of that glory simply by knowing what it is to ride fast and hard. He belongs to the fraternity of the road, whose membership is free, international and democratic. Cycle-racing is a passport to the continent: I raced in Spain, Belgium and Ireland. To become a member, all you need to have done is to have ridden as if you meant it. And if you achieve any distinction as an amateur racer, it is likely that you will at some point find yourself lining up with professionals. Few in cycling succeed in living their dream, but many can touch the hem of the cloth in which those dreams are woven. Anyone can cycle the route of the Tour.

Arguably, the physical demands racers make of themselves are damaging rather than beneficial for their health. Some say that each Tour de France takes a year off a racer's life. And yet, when you race, you feel that that is what life is for, its whole aim and purpose. All racing cyclists, including amateurs as I was, may be addicted to the opiates which the brain releases to tamp down the discomfort of extreme exertion, but more they are junkies for the subculture of their sport, its secret knowledge and fraternal spirit. Much more than endorphins, cycling's myths are what they cannot give up. They are not looking to recruit or convert anyone else. Why are we doing this? a racer will mutter to another as the peloton passes a country pub where people are sitting outside eating lunch and drinking beer. The answer is the desire to be different, to excel at something very difficult, and to belong.

Racers belong to a secret society. As they pass one another on the road on training rides, racers will acknowledge each other without taking their hands off the bars by a flick of the fingers or nod of the head. Riding in groups, they have a modest but sufficient vocabulary of signals and phrases. A hand waved behind the back indicates to other riders an upcoming obstacle or hazard. Where a breakaway group is sharing the work of pace-setting, a rider might indicate that his turn on the front is done just by a twitch of his elbow. On a narrow country road a cry of *Oil up!* warns of an approaching motor vehicle. Terms from French and Italian fill the cyclist's lexicon. A circuit race may contain several intermediate sprints, known as *primes*, for prizes or points. A young aspirant who sets too keen a pace at the foot of a long climb may be reprimanded *Piano! Piano!* (*Softly! Softly!*) by a more experienced rider. The moment of true thrill is biding your time until the moment is right, then launching yourself up the road to leave the bunch for dust. But like as not, you will soon be joined by others. In a break your rivals become temporary companions and allies in the effort to maintain the gap back to the bunch. Usually someone will take charge and get the break working together, riding *through and off* in turn to keep the pace high while sharing the work of being on the front. But eventually there will come the moment, often on the bell-lap, when your partners in the break will start to make their calculations about how far remains to the line, who still has good legs, and where to strike out on their own. This will be the last desperate throw of the dice. To escape the escape, that is the endgame of the bicycle race.

The great escapes are etched on my memory. They were the golden moments of my cycling career, moments I often relived, replaying them in my head like video highlights. These images remain, but as, over time, they grow blurred and indistinct, they hover ambiguously between a life I still crave but can no longer have and a life that looks so strange and unfamiliar as to belong to another person. They are visions of flight into a parallel world, a world which I sometimes miss and mourn yet also feel grateful finally to have escaped.

Stage 1

Get a bicycle. You will not regret it, if you live.
— Mark Twain

For a time there were four bicycles in my life.

I had a training bike. At a casual glance you would say it was a racer. It was built with relaxed angles, with eyelets for a rack and mudguards, so that it could double as a tourer. The frame was made from Reynolds 531C tubing and painted a metallic British racing green. The maker's name, Cougar, was printed in white decals down the front of the forks.

There was also my pale blue track bike, which I stored in a rusty steel container behind the Herne Hill cycle track in south London where I did all my track-riding. It was not a thing of beauty, but with Miche chainset and 24-spoke Mavic rims, it was serviceable enough.

And of course there was my racing bike. Like many bikies, I did not have the money to assemble my dream bicycle all at once. In its final form my racer was worth more than £1,500. It was an evolving thing; I collected it bit by bit. The Roberts frame was bought from a man who worked in a bikeshop and, tempted by his trade discounts, had overextended his credit. I got it for £600, a good price. It was metallic black, and the top-of-the-range Shimano components it came with were worth the price alone. But as I rode more and found my style, I came to realise that it was an inch and a half too small for me. Wheel rims, brake shoes, even chain rings wear out and get replaced, but the frame is always the soul of the machine.

At last the day came when I could afford a made-to-measure frame. This was like ordering a bespoke suit. I had to fill in a complex form that the north-east-based frame-builder, Phil Donohue, faxed down to the shop: height and weight, inside leg and torso measurements, arm length from shoulder to cuff and elbow to finger. It was to be made out of Reynolds 653, double-butted and silver-soldered for the perfect combination of lightness and strength.

When the frame finally arrived, six weeks later, it gleamed immaculate in its metallic colours – the red and blue of my club, the Vélo Club de Londres. It seemed impossibly light, even when fully kitted out with Dura-ace hubs, brakes and chainset, Mavic rims, Cinelli bars with cork tape, and Rolls saddle. Stiff, comfortable and fast, the Donohue was everything you could want from a racer. As soon as you mounted it, snapping into the clipless pedals, you felt its coherence and integrity, but above all its pent-up go, its desire for speed.

Later, I also owned a mountain bike. An off-the-peg Trek dating from the days before V-brakes and suspension, sturdy but nothing special. Considering I once regarded mountain biking as a perversion of the cyclist's true vocation, I got good use from it.

Today my bikes are gathering dust on top of the road grime they collected the last times I used them. The track bike is gone altogether, bequeathed to clubmates and cannibalised for wheels and parts. Those that remain I could not ride now – the tyres have perished, the inner tubes parched as the sloughed-off skin of a snake.

Only the racer, always the best cared for and now disassembled and bagged in the attic, remains pristine. But with every passing year it becomes more of a museum piece. Each season the bike makers introduce new styles and materials for their topflight racing frames – last year it was aluminium, this year it's carbon fibre, next year it might be titanium. This constant updating of the racing bike, dictated in part by new technologies and in part by fashion, combines with a relentless marketing-led evolution of bike components. No matter Phil Donohue's fine artisanship with steel alloy, my old racer would now look quaint and obsolete.

I sometimes wonder what these relics will mean to my children when I am older. What will they tell them about my former life? I remember the thrill of discovery when my brother and I found my father's old cricket gear in the back of a cupboard. He had been a fine amateur player. We had spent numberless Saturday and Sunday afternoons playing beside the boundary in those pretty tree-framed cricket grounds that are scattered over rural southern England. Among my earliest memories there is our mother, sitting on a rug some way from the pavilion – that place where we rarely ventured: it belonged to the players, large men in cable-knit sweaters who laughed loud.

I wonder what she thought of those long afternoons, our mother. Whether she liked the tranquillity of the countryside, the lazy pace of the game and its atmosphere of cultivated irrelevance, and the amiable diffidence of conversation with the other players' wives. Or did the coming of summer bring with it a secret dread? Those long afternoons stretching out, not as a succession of gentle pleasures, but as a series of dreary hurdles to be endured in the company of two small children who had to be kept amused, while she herself was a captive spectator at a game which held little interest for her. Did she feel that deep inner fatigue then, which, I know now, belongs specially to new parents as the thought dawns: so this is my life now?

Nothing would have given my father more pleasure than for me to follow in his cricketing footsteps. I played in the school sides, but as I grew older it became apparent that I had neither the talent nor the confidence to make it my game. I moved away from team games and for a while focused my efforts on the solo sports of tennis and golf. But by the time I went to university I had virtually abandoned competitive sports. I played a few desultory games of hockey for my college, smoking roll-ups in the changing room before and after the game.

My father contained his disappointment. He said little of it, only sometimes liked to remind me of my cricketing potential – which perhaps had always been greater in his imagining, and definitely was so now in his regret for its being unfulfilled. It took me a while to understand this. As with any oft-repeated narrative, those stories about ourselves which have the character of myth, that constitute our kinship in ways of which we are largely unconscious, are subject to subtle distortions. It is easy to invest too much in the fictions that make life tolerable.

I don't remember much about my first bike, but I do remember learning to ride it. Properly, without stabilisers. I was five or six. From the start, perhaps, cycling was tinged with romance, for I was coached by the young French student then staying with us. Dominique was part student, part family friend. I learnt to ride on the sloping grass lawn of our back garden, accompanied by her exclamations – '*Allons-y! Très bien! Attention!*' – while I concentrated so hard on balancing that I would forget to use the brakes and veer into the shrubs.

I was timorous to begin with. Dominique quickly ran out of patience with me and my lessons soon consisted not so much of coaching as shaming. I was old enough to ride a bike properly, 'like a big boy, without zese leetle wheels'. Finally stung into a more courageous effort, I forced myself wobblingly forwards.

But once I could ride my bike, there was no holding me back, and off I charged. The sense of liberation as the ground began to blur was as palpable as the wind rushing past my face – the joy of speed so expressively captured in the French word *vélo* (and so typically ignored by the English-empiricist description, *bicycle*).

Flying down the pavement outside our drive on a bicycle was soon the distilled essence of fun, the risk of a fall merely adding to the thrill. The playing fields behind our house, with their tarmacadamed tennis courts, concrete paths and big grass banks where the land had been levelled, made a vast adventure playground safely away from the road. In summer the mowers would leave vast clumps of cut grass like miniature hay bales. The kids from our road would heap these clippings into a big pile and shape it like a ramp at the bottom of one of these steep banks. Then we'd hurtle down, at what felt like terminal speed, hit the bottom of the bank with a scary stomach-lurching whump and shoot over the grass ramp.

You had a fraction of a second before you were airborne to remember to try and pull up on the bars so you would land safely on the back wheel or both wheels simultaneously. Even at the height of our daring, none of us ever achieved a jump of more than three or four feet, but on our small-wheeled bikes, it was enough. And if you landed badly off-line or front-wheel first, there was always the risk of skinning your shins on the pedals or belly-flopping in the hard earth and winding yourself.

I fell once not riding, but just running down one of those bank. Legs flailing, cartoonishly unable to keep pace with my gathering momentum, I went flat on my face at the bottom and came up, not in pain, but aware that something uncanny and queasy-making had happened to my hand. When I looked down there was a deep inch-and-a-half gash at the base of my thumb. It oozed red, and I saw the cut was as clean as one carved by a scalpel – except there was the minutely serated edge of a long blade of grass poking out from one end. I pulled out the grass, fascinated and horrified, and then, as the bleeding increased, the red stuff running ticklishly round my wrist, I hoped it needed stitches. It did not, but it left a scar, an ad hoc extension to my lifeline.

One of my friends in the playing fields had a Chipper, a scaled-down version of the Chopper. With high-rise handle-bars, Easy Rider-style leatherette seat and centre-mounted three-speed gearshift, the Chopper was tough and cool. Mostly you'd see kids from the estates riding them up and down kerbs and pulling wheelies. The Chipper was its younger brother.

We asked our parents for them, knowing in advance the answer. Sure enough, we were told they were *not safe*. We knew that what they really meant was that Choppers weren't meant for children from good families. The Chopper represented enough of an affront to the responsible adult idea of what a proper bike should look like that there had been concerned stories in the papers about how children were being maimed en masse because these newfangled bikes were inherently unstable. But for a kid in the seventies, all you cared was that they looked cool and were brilliant for doing wheelies.

To pull a good wheelie, where you pedalled along keeping the front wheel up in the air, took real flair and skill. The trick was to practise where no one could watch your mistakes. I was never very good at wheelies, but then I never had a Chopper. The first stirrings of teen rebellion came via another set of wheels: the skateboard craze of the late seventies. Scandalously, I blew my entire post-office savings on the best board I could afford. I worked doggedly at my 180s and 360s, but I was never going to be one of the cool kids who could pull a crowd just to see them ride the white bowl at the Southwick skatepark, near Shoreham – the cement garden where I skinned my knees and elbows.

I moved on to fishing, fired by the vision of living off the land offered by my favourite book, *The Survivor's Handbook*. I loved its unwritten premise: the adventure of being shipwrecked, marooned or lost. It spoke to a boy's dream of wilderness living, of looking after himself alone in a world full of promise and threat where he had to know how to skin a rabbit and where there would be no one to tell him to clean his teeth. So inspired, I learnt to overcome my squeamishness – to spear a ragworm through its rapacious mouth and neatly kebab a section of its body on the hook. It was still a long time before I made my first and only catch, from the pier in Penzance during a family holiday in Cornwall. It was a whiting, weighing perhaps two pounds. It flapped disconsolately on the line while I reeled it in. As it came over the parapet I saw it was hooked in the belly. I felt a cheat, that I had landed it by some low stratagem. Rigor mortis stiffened the fish inside the plastic bag I carried home. I could hardly bear to look at it, let alone eat it. It went in the bin the next day.

These things had begun in such a flurry of enthusiasm that I was like a person possessed, impossible to gainsay or divert from my purpose. In my head I had always some idealised vision of how that purpose would be realised. But once that perfect experience failed to materialise, disillusion crept in. All my projects finally petered out with a sense of disappointment that was, like the original ideal, elusive and hard to name. Through my teenage years, the one constant that survived this succession of crazes – though I never recognised it as such – was my bike. It was often disregarded, neglected, abandoned for months at a time, but it was always there: my Raleigh Jubilee.

Silver framed, with red, white and blue trim, my Raleigh was one of a limited edition made to mark the Queen's Silver Jubilee. My dad had bought it for me second-hand, when it must have been only two or three years old. In time I found a silver-coloured pump with tricolour bands to match the scratched decals on the frame. I replaced the peeling black vinyl tape on the handlebars with fresh royal-blue cloth tape. My brother was gratifyingly envious.

Raleigh was *the* name in serious bikes, and this was a real racer with drop handlebars and ten – ten! – gears. I used to keep the chain on the big front ring all the time, because I thought the small cog was for sissies. So I rode it as though it were a five-gear bike. It felt like the real thing: I would crouch low, with my head down and elbows tucked in, and fly down hills as though I were an alpine skier.

You had to watch out in the wet. The bike's chrome-rimmed wheels became slippery and made braking a frantic white-knuckle business. You would squeeze and nothing would happen; you'd squeeze harder and still nothing would happen; then suddenly the brake blocks would start to bite, and if you managed not to skid, at last you'd come to a juddering halt.

For all its special edition decals, like most Raleigh products of that era, the Jubilee was essentially a mass-market bicycle. It was aimed at a domestic consumer who would have considered more than £200 an extravagant fortune to spend on a bicycle. It never occurred to me that bikes could get any better than this, with its sturdy but crude steel frame that sent every bump and wrinkle in the rode jarring through your hands and buttocks.

There were no cyclists in our family, or among my parents' friends, that I knew of. None of us would have been even dimly aware that the Tour de France had come to Britain in 1974 for a single stage. Given the status of cycling, it did not prove an auspicious decision. Road-racing in Britain was probably at its lowest ebb at any time in the century. Track-racing still enjoyed some small currency, thanks largely to the legendary exploits of Reg Harris. But even these were gradually fading into the fog of folk memory. Only if it were a slow day on the BBC's *Grandstand* would highlights of the national track championships make a short item before the half-time football scores.

For years, road-racing had been virtually outlawed because of its inconvenience to motor traffic, and the only form of competitive cycling that survived was time-trialling. Time-trialling is, to put it mildly, an unspectacular form of racing in which competitors are sent off at one minute intervals to ride against the clock on a given course, generally out and back down the same road, often some lonely stretch of dual carriageway. Because of its dubious legality, time trials took place in the early hours of the morning so that they would be all over by 8 a.m. when the local constabulary was still finishing breakfast. As a further precaution, whenever upcoming time trials were advertised in the cycling press, the location of the particular route to be used was disguised by giving it a codename which sounded like a road number but wasn't. The semi-underground

17

status of time-trialling meant that the tradition of road-racing in Britain was kept alive, if only obscurely, by a clandestine brotherhood. It was a version of cycle-sport that seemed to breed dour, phlegmatic, insular types: the type of person that gets up at 4.30 a.m. on a Sunday morning to ride a 25 or a 50 is not the soul of the party on Saturday nights.

Time-trialling remains part of every racing cyclist's repertoire, for almost every stage race contains at least one time trial stage. Because it is a pure test of a solo rider's speed, the *contre la montre* is sometimes known as the race of truth. For that reason if no other, Britain's time-trialling tradition does have the merit that it finds out the truly talented rider. And so, as if by an accident of nature, Britain always seemed to produce the occasional cyclist who emerged to make a career as a professional on the Continent. In the sixties, the great white hope was Tommy Simpson, before his untimely death from amphetamine-induced heart failure on the searing moonscape slopes of Mont Ventoux during the 1967 Tour. Though less a household name, Barry Hoban was another British rider who found a place in the peloton. He was riding in the 1974 Tour when the race entourage arrived by ferry at Plymouth.

Since the *rosbifs* had no concept that you might actually close roads for a bicycle race, they had arranged for the Tour riders to compete over a stretch of just completed but unopened A-road in Devon. Whereas the Tour usually processed through an unfolding landscape of French countryside where entire towns and villages would turn out to cheer their heroes past, here it was reduced to a grim chase up and down a windswept piece of dual carriageway with scant spectators. It was a very seventies, very British cock-up: the riders complained bitterly, and the Tour did not return for twenty years.

I saw my first Tour de France when I was fifteen. It was

18

the school holidays, the end of July, and I was staying with Dominique's family in Paris. I had just done my O-levels. On paper my French was not bad, but I was at an age where trying to articulate anything, even in my mother tongue, had become a kind of medieval ordeal for me. No doubt despairing of things to do with the taciturn teenager I had become, Dominique took me one Sunday to see the end of the Tour de France, its climactic stage on the Champs-Elysées. We joined the crowds at the Arc de Triomphe end of the grand avenue where the riders race up, then brake sharply, cautiously describe a 180° turn round the central reservation, and then charge back down the other side for another circuit.

The crowds were a dozen deep at the barriers, and although we tried to squeeze in, I do not remember seeing even a single cyclist. While trying to worm my way through, I became separated from Dominique, who was holding back from the worst of the crush. It was a warm afternoon, made hotter still in among all the confined bodies. I felt a pressure behind me, like someone else trying to push in. Though hemmed in on all sides, I tried to make way, but instead of squeezing by, the mass remained pinned to me. I decided to stand my ground instead, assuming it was a sway of body upon body in the crowd, a wave created somewhere else which would soon ebb.

But the pressure kept up, insistently bearing in on me. Beginning to feel uncomfortable and slightly annoyed, I turned my head to see where it was coming from. A tallish, heavily built, middle-aged man in a well-pressed short-sleeved shirt was next to me. He was wearing Reactolite shades, lighter at the bottom of the lens than at the top, and as I looked round he caught my eye and smiled.

— *Bonjour*.

— *Bonjour*, I replied, turning away and wishing earnestly for the first time that there were some cyclists to see.

— *Vous êtes allemand?* he asked.

— *Non. Je suis anglais.*

— Ah, Eng-leesh. And do you live here?

— *Non*, I said, determined not to break my resolution to speak only French, but for once grateful for the language barrier. — *Je me rends visite à mes amis.*

— Are you staying near here?

Just then, I became aware of Dominique's voice hailing me from behind.

— *Matthieu! . . . Matthieu, c'est fini, je crois. Allons-y!*

Relieved, I made my way through the throng to where she had waved from.

— *Bien. Tu as fait un nouvel ami?* she asked, looking at me with the corners of her mouth upturned in an ironic smile.

— *Oui. Un peu trop*, I said, pulling a face. She laughed, and I allowed myself to realise for the first time why – or rather, what – the man in the shades had been pressing up against me.

Two years later I learned to drive. By then I had finished growing. I was seventeen, brushing six foot and cultivating sideburns to help me get served in pubs. My bike, the Raleigh, was stuck at the back of the garage, gathering dust. I had decided that it was too small for me. It seemed in any case a childish thing. For me, the car was king. Who wouldn't rather drive? To clinch the matter, who would want to go out with a guy without a car?

I had access to my mum's car. The problem was I still didn't have a girlfriend. There had been a couple of near misses, but my luck did not really begin to change until at last I became a student and got back on my old Raleigh. De-mothballed, preserved in the perpetual youth of its 1977 colours, it still seemed like a great bike. Compared to the creaking, rusty sit-up-and-begs that had served several generations of Cambridge students and which it was almost redundant to lock up since theft would have been an act of charity, my Raleigh was a speed-machine. Not that anyone cared but me.

I had started going to the meetings of the student Left in a room above the bar in King's College. I didn't have any very coherent politics, so I kept quiet and listened to the politicos who had their positions all worked out. All I really knew was that I was afraid of nuclear war. I joined CND and went to a big demonstration in Barrow-in-Furness to protest against Trident submarines. And went on sitting quietly at the meetings, rolling weedy little cigarettes from a half-ounce packet of Old Holborn. Practically everyone smoked, it seemed. By the end of the lunch hour, a grey-brown pall hung over the room. Ruth told me later that she had thought I looked cool and intimidating, sitting there smoking roll-ups with my bleached hair and second-hand mac. I found this hard to believe.

I noticed Ruth early in these meetings. It was impossible not to. She was tall, and she talked. She had a big bush of curly hair that went out and up in every direction, unless she had succeeded in packing it under a beret, which she sometimes did. She often wore a big dress with a smudgy black and white pattern, topped off with a little knitted pink cardigan. They hid her figure entirely, but she was still tall enough to look good.

She had an unusual face: a full mouth with regular teeth, a broad, flat nose and small, slightly Asiatic eyes. She was not pretty in any conventional sense, but compelling to look at; someone with presence. She said more than any other woman who came to these meetings and when she spoke, her lips curled back over her teeth and sometimes her voice shook a little. She could be nervous, but it never stopped her having a say. She was stroppy but charismatic.

We were beginning to move in the same social orbit. We first talked properly at a weekly Labour Club disco at a cramped dive just off the Market Square in Cambridge. It was called Rosa's since, naturally, if Rosa Luxemburg had been a Cambridge student in 1984, she would have deejayed for the Labour students. I sensed Ruth's volatility, and wondered afterwards if I'd been too acquiescent, too quick to agree and seek identity, rather than assert myself. But she had responded that way too. Neither of us stayed late. I went back to my room, filled with surprise at how wrong was my assumption that she was prickly and unapproachable, and buoyed up with hope that we might get to know each other better. But this would be different: I was determined not to rush things.

I did not have to wait too long. A week later someone we both knew threw a party in the cellar rooms of his college. There was a small gang of us, and we danced together all evening. The music was too loud for anyone to talk. Normally, I hated this: I would get bored with dancing and crave verbal interaction, but on this night I didn't care. Ruth looked fantastic. She was wearing eyeliner and bright red lipstick. I'd never seen her in make-up. Best of all, she was wearing a killer tartan mini-skirt and black tights.

It wasn't late when the party wound up, so our group became a small party back at the house Ruth shared. It was only a ten-minute walk and not all of us had bikes, so Ruth wheeled hers. It was a sensible, three-speed girl's bike, with a white wire basket in front for carrying files and books.

We all drank tea and ate toast with peanut butter in the

kitchen. Gradually, the evening wound down and, one by one, the friends left and Ruth's housemates took off to bed. Finally, there was just Ruth, me and this one other guy left in the kitchen. Ruth started washing-up, but he was too drunk to take a hint, so after a while she broke off from the dishes and efficiently ushered him out. Then we were alone. Suddenly, I was paralysed with nerves.

A silence settled over the kitchen. Ruth, still finishing the washing-up, her back turned to me, asked:

— So, do you want to stay?

We spent the weeks and months that followed getting to know one another, nearly splitting up several times, slowly falling in love. Being in a relationship was a novelty I felt utterly unprepared for – a crash course in emotional literacy. No one had ever explained how bizarre and difficult it was to be intimately involved with another person. But by the beginning of our final year, we had reached some kind of stable state. Unfashionable though it then was in our circle, we were a couple.

We cycled everywhere together, first in Cambridge and then later in London, after we had both graduated and found work. Like everything else we had to learn about each other, this required patience, strategy and compromise. Ruth was always complaining that I would ride too fast. Sure enough, if I went in front, no matter how slowly I pedalled, I always seemed to be leaving her behind. I suspected, of course, that she was soft-pedalling just to prove her point. Come on, you keep slowing down, I protested once or twice. But this was met with robust denial. Sometimes, I would try riding alongside to be companionable, but it seemed to make her nervous about traffic or cramp her style. If a car came in sight, she would shoo me away. In the end, it worked best if I let her ride in front. As long as she set the pace, we bowled along at a brisk enough rate, and I was happy and comfortable.

Stage 2

Socialism can only arrive on a bicycle.

— José Antonio Viera Gallo

After we moved to London, Ruth and I lived for the first few months in a flat above her sister's in Kentish Town. It belonged to a film-maker who lived mostly in the United States and it hadn't been decorated since sometime in the mid-seventies. The lounge carpet was deep-pile brown beneath the smoked glass coffee table. There was a magnificent sheepskin Afghan coat in a closet and the walls were decorated with large portraits of teenage Indian prostitutes whose melancholy gaze was hard to live with. After a few days we took down the pictures in the bedroom.

I rode a bike to work, down through Camden, past St Pancras, into Bloomsbury. I had finally abandoned my battered Raleigh, leaving it with a friend in Cambridge who, still languishing in student poverty, seemed glad to have it. In truth I was not much better off. After graduating, I had surprised myself by being accepted for the first proper job I applied for, as an editorial assistant to a reference publisher in Cambridge. Almost everyone there was a former university student who had started a PhD, taken this job to support themselves when their grant ran out, and never left. They were all intelligent, interesting people, but their collective predicament filled me with dread. I knew I had to escape.

When, a few months later, I was offered a job in London with Lawrence & Wishart – established 1936, the house publisher of the British Communist Party – I celebrated by upping my overdraft to splash out £200 on a new road bike, which I bought from F. W. Evans in The Cut at Waterloo. I was still a virtual stranger to bikeshops but I knew enough to tell that Evans was a place for serious cyclists. The way you could tell was that it didn't have any lines of cheap kids' bikes out front. The bike I bought was Evans's own brand; this seemed sensible to me since I didn't know anything about the bewildering array of non-proprietary makes. Its colour was brilliant white, with a frame made of 501 tubing. The gears and brakes – Shimano 105s – were made of light steel alloy. With its elegantly curved shapes and recessed Allen bolts, the rear derailleur was incomparably superior to the Jubilee's old Huret one. The chain barely murmured as it climbed from one cog to another. The wheels too were alloy. They braked much better in the wet and I could not believe how tough they were. At first, whenever I hit a pothole I would stop and pull over with a sickened feeling, convinced that the rim must be dented or buckled. I had sometimes taken a hammer to the rims of my old Raleigh in a rudimentary attempt to straighten a kink. But these alloy wheels seemed almost indestructible. For the first time in my life I had a bike that I was determined to take care of, to keep as pristine as I could.

My white Evans lived in the communal hall, alongside Ruth's bike – the same bike she had had as a student. I pedalled to work via Bayswater, along the top of Hyde Park and down the length of Oxford Street, weaving past the buses, dodging the pedestrians and U-turning taxis. The air was full of fumes and diesel soot. Although I soon learnt the skill that becomes automatic for urban cyclists – of tasting the air before you breathe it and holding your breath if it's foul – I still found I had to wash my face when I reached the office, not only to wipe away the perspiration but also to remove the smuts.

On the way home one day, after about two months of travelling this route, I was hit by a taxi as it wheeled suddenly round. Clearly the collision was not my fault: he was pulled over to the left and had not indicated at all. But my inexperience – a lack of anticipation of others' possible errors – undoubtedly had something to do with it. The driver was a sandy-haired man in his forties with teeth so bad it was a struggle not to stare. He was shaken up himself and talked fifteen to the dozen as he picked me up, dusted me down, and took me and my bike home in his cab. I was not much hurt, although one cheek was glowing hot pink and my jaw ached from where I'd hit the side of his cab. I did my best to put him at ease; he seemed almost more in shock than me.

We swapped addresses and a week later I sent him a bill for repair of my bent forks and buckled front wheel. I heard nothing. Eventually I called him up. He had had my letter, but he had also lost any anxiety about having his carriage licence revoked.

— You must be joking. A bicycle wheel don't cost forty quid, mate.

I said I could send him the receipt from the bikeshop, but he wasn't having any of that.

— G'urn, get out of 'ere, he said cheerily as he put the phone down on me.

*   *   *

I had not had to go far, at least, to get my bike mended. One of the local landmarks was the bikeshop in All Saint's Road. All Saint's Road, W11 was the frontline: its reputation as a drug-dealing street attracted heavy policing, which in turn made it a stage for ritual confrontation between black activists and the authorities. At one time officers were stationed in pairs on every corner all the way down the street as part of a saturation policing policy.

Ninon's bicycle shop was an incongruous sight among the run-down row of shops and shabby cafés. Ninon hardly seemed to sell bicycles at all. There was no showroom and there were no bikes on display. Instead the business seemed to function by selling parts and doing repairs. Downstairs was a basement where a frame-builder worked. Sometimes when you were in there, he would emerge blinkingly for a cup of coffee or just to chat with Ninon and the lads who worked for her. Ignorant of why anyone would order a frame separately from a frame-builder, I never ventured down into his domain. I imagined it as a cramped, airless cellar supplied solely by artificial light and smelling infernally of brazing solder.

Upstairs was airy and friendly. Ninon, the owner, was a short, stout woman of indeterminate age – it might have been anywhere between thirty and fifty. She smiled readily but was reticent with customers. The paradox of Ninon's shop was that, despite her shyness, it was a tremendously social place. People would stop by just to hang out. I, too, found myself inventing spurious errands that would take me by the shop.

Besides her, there were in her employ – as there eternally are in every bikeshop in the land – a couple of slim lads who worked as mechanics and retail assistants. But unlike lads in other bikeshops, who have utter contempt for someone who doesn't know their headset from their crank arm, Ninon's boys never looked askance at the bikes people brought in. They didn't tell you that it wasn't worth their while to change a gear cable because what you needed was a whole new mechanism. They just did what was necessary to get you on your way again, with no fuss or tongue-clicking. If they were not too busy, then for a nominal charge they would cheerfully mend your puncture while you waited.

Bikeshop boys take jobs in bikeshops because they love bikes and they get a good discount. But what they love most is playing with bikes and riding them, not selling them and, worse, answering questions about whether they've got a new nut to go on this bit, and do they know why the gears are making this noise, and, by the way, do they have a set of allen keys to lend. For most of these young men, the compensation for the boredom of the retail routine and the frustration of dealing with all those idiotic customers is the opportunity to humiliate them in a multitude of under-the-counter ways.

Ninon's boys were very different, betraying no impatience at the average customer's phobic ignorance about how bikes work and what to do when they don't. They just loved bikes. One, a fresh-faced young man named Tim, told me about the *fixed* he liked to ride: I had never heard of such a thing – a bike without gears, this seemed a truly radical idea when almost everyone equated the degree of sophistication of bike and cyclist by the number of gears they had. But Tim explained how riding a fixed, where there is no freewheel, so that as long as the bike is moving you must be pedalling, developed a more fluid pedalling style. Even the notion that one could pedal in a certain style, and that different styles were possible, was revelatory. Most weeks, then, I would find an excuse to drop into the shop to buy an inner tube or new brake blocks, but in reality to renew my membership of their circle. Gradually I realised that this club of cycle enthusiasts was one to which I wanted to belong.

— Have you seen those couriers in their cycle shorts? said my boss, Jim Kellagher, standing and looking out of the window in the shopfront of our shabby Bloomsbury office.

I looked up from the old manual typewriter where I had been bashing away viciously, a key at a time, at the warehouse order-form. My stupid typewriter always seemed to need a new ribbon. I hated those forms with their double carbon copies.

Lawrence & Wishart celebrated its fiftieth anniversary in 1986, the year before I started there. I had little Marx and less Lenin then, but I was an earnest student caught up in the romance of communism. Of course, I knew in outline about 1956, when many members left the Party in protest, but it never occurred to me that 1986 was the thirtieth anniversary of that much less glorious episode in communist history.

— Don't leave much to the imagination, do they? Kellagher went on, hands thrust in pockets, grinning. Nothing tickled him quite so much as an opportunity to make a salacious remark.

— I expect you'll have a pair next.

Distracted by the frolics of a group of foreign students across the road, Kellagher left off his taunting about cycle shorts and I was, for once, reprieved. At this stage, I was a tempting target for Kellagher. I was still on a big pure-socialism kick which was quite extreme: it was one thing to despise City traders flaunting their new-minted wealth in their Porsches, but it was another thing entirely to regard Lycra cycle shorts as a symptom of bourgeois decadence just because they were fashionable. But that was my official view. To reinforce it, on Saturdays I bought the hardline *Morning*

Star, no doubt doubling its circulation in Notting Hill. I had to keep quiet about this – it was not done to be seen reading that sectarian rag at work during the week.

For all the shame and recrimination that went with the word Communist, it still contained a tattered, embattled sense of pride. By some strange compensatory logic, defeat would always be alchemised into victory – or at least a reason to go on with the struggle. That was the quixotic theme that gave the Party its unique flavour of flawed nobility which drew me to it. Britons generally are said to love a loser, but no one knew how to celebrate losing like us British commies. Here was the real romance: to identify with the underdog in history was always to find yourself on the losing side.

I was what you would call a joiner, someone who likes to sign up to an organisation, a collectivity larger than himself; someone who in some way needs that way of belonging. But then, one was hardly likely to take out a Communist Party card if that were not the case; it was not something casually undertaken, like becoming a member at your local video store.

Three months later I found myself fishing a pair of cycling shorts out of the sale bin at Ninon's shop in All Saints Road. Perhaps it had been the rain-soaked charity ride when I had worn cut-off jeans which provided the excuse I needed, but now the logic of owning a pair of Lycra shorts with a chamois insert to pad my contact with the saddle had become inescapable. The more time I spent in and out of Ninon's shop, the more I surrendered myself to the idea that cycle shorts actually looked pretty cool. It was a matter of days before I was riding to work in them. In my fluorescent-yellow *Marxism Today* bike-bag I would carry a pair of boxer shorts and jeans to change into amid the dusty boxes in the basement.

For two or three years running, a group of friends and I took part in a ride organised by the Nicaragua Solidarity Campaign which went from London to Oxford. One year Ninon's boys did the ride too. I didn't see them, but we spoke later in the shop about how much we had enjoyed the route through the Chiltern Hills. Tim had ridden his fixed, of course.

I became eclectic in my causes. There was a very popular ride to raise money for the London Lighthouse AIDS hospice that finished in the grounds of a stately home near Box Hill in Surrey. By then, I had done enough of those rides to make the task of collecting sponsorship more arduous than the ride itself. I had not quite realised this, but the cause was becoming immaterial. It was the cycling that carried me along.

After the start, I never stayed with Ruth or my friends for long. They always seemed happy to dawdle along, while I wanted to press on. There was no competition: everyone set off at different times and rode at different speeds and no one was clocking your time at the end. But I found it almost physically uncomfortable to have to ride too slowly. It was not that I wanted to race against anyone, but just to push myself.

That was how I met Mick. We were riding at the same speed.

He was on an old Raleigh that was a dirty lemon colour. He looked of similar height and weight to me, and the frame of his bike looked a little small for him. We kept slipping in and out of each other's view. Sometimes one of us would get ahead, sometimes the other. I tried speeding up a bit, to see if that would shake him off, but it didn't. There he was, doggedly pedalling away just a few yards behind me. After about twenty minutes this private race became unsustainable and some acknowledgement became necessary.

— Have you done this ride before?

— No. You?

Another junction came up, with a bottleneck of riders waiting to cross. When the chance came, we sprinted away from the slow-moving pack, but (it was now understood) not from each other.

— So what do you do?

— I work as a courier.

I was impressed, and slightly intimidated. Cycle couriers were a new and exotic breed on the streets of London. Some of them had weird low-profile bikes and wore the full figure-hugging kit. Others rode the new mountain bikes, coolly distressed so they already look tanked. They tended to opt for a kind of urban-guerrilla anarchist chic.

This guy looked more like the former type, but more approachable, less of a poseur. We felt comfortable riding at each other's speed; enough of a challenge without being over-taxing. I have often thought since that whatever else Mick and I had in common, the most fundamental thing about our friendship was that we were almost perfectly matched for speed. Differences came and went – sometimes our levels of fitness and stamina varied, at other times the circumstances of our lives diverged – but there was always the knowledge that we could get on our bikes and find that, without even thinking about it, we were riding at the same tempo.

By the time we reached the grounds of Polesden Lacey, where the ride ended, I was pleasantly tired. We arrived far ahead of the friends I had set off with, so Mick and I sat on the grass in the sunshine next to our bikes and drank a pint of the potent, hoppy beer supplied from the Workers' Beer Co. tent. I felt a warm, tingling sensation in my legs that was amplified by the brew. We made small talk about cycling, politics and beer, until distracted by the piecemeal arrival of our respective parties.

Though mildly irritated that I hadn't waited at the last checkpoint, Ruth put up with my explanation that I had made a new friend I wanted to stick with to the finish. She knew how I was – how reluctant I was to ride at an artificially slow pace. It seemed something she would simply have to accept about me.

Before we all left for the railway station, Mick came over and we swapped telephone numbers.

— We should go for a ride sometime. Just on our own.

— Yeah, that would be great.

At that moment, suffused with comradeliness, I still believed it was the package of social rides for good causes that I liked. But what Mick instinctively recognised in me was someone else who was really into the cycling. Just the cycling.

My first pair of shorts from Ninon's shop did not last long. The Lycra was low-grade and the elasthane soon lost its stretch, so that the smooth, skin-tight effect was gone and the shorts looked like something I'd knitted myself. Every time I washed them – which I had to do almost daily otherwise the chamois started smelling like the old goat it had indeed once been – they turned to cardboard. An application of Vaseline (in place of expensive chamois cream) helped with the stiffness, but after you had been riding for a while, it made the shorts feel as though you were wearing a greasy nappy.

In the old days, even into the 1970s, all cycle clothing had been made of wool. Before the Lycra revolution this made sense: woven wool was form-fitting and stretchy; it was also breathable, hard-wearing, and able to retain bodyheat even when soaked. Still, the handwashing must have been hell and the jerseys would have been hot and prickly to wear in summer. Then, if they could afford it, racers would wear jerseys made of silk. I once borrowed an old club jersey in silk: its colours had faded but it still felt deliciously cool against the skin. It was so light that I felt exposed, almost naked, when wearing it. A shirt like that could only have been worn for racing on summer's warmest days and longest evenings.

Before shorts had chamois inserts, the early riders of the Tour de France improvised. The legend went that they would buy a cheap cut of steak from a local butcher in the morning. Ready for the off, they'd stick the slab of beef down their shorts and sit on it like a cushion. They'd ride like that all day – tenderising the meat with their motion, marinading it in their sweat – then hand it to the hotel chef in the evening with the instruction that it needed only a minute on each side. In those days, protein rather than pasta was thought the diet of champions. And riders en route were as apt to accept a quick brandy from the bar in the square as to fill their bottles from the fountain.

Shorts became longer with the advent of Lycra, at least for the practical reason that they would ride up and bunch if it weren't for rubberised grips around the hem which held the shorts' legs down to where your thighs began to taper to your knees. When you look now at pictures of Eddy Merckx at his peak in the early seventies, you see an unfamiliarly long flash of shank with all but the top three or four inches of thigh exposed.

That little strip of nakedness speaks of an era of raw competition, a kind of sleeves-rolled-up, sons-of-toil physicality that has been refined out of existence among today's scientifically prepared professional athletes. The professionals of the 1960s and earlier, it is generally accepted among the cycling fraternity, were the real hard men. Like any other sport, cycling has its version of the myth that we shall not see their like again. Somehow the black and white photography that recorded riders like Fausto Coppi, Gino Bartali, Charly Gaul and Louison Bobet, and a numberless regiment of all-but-forgotten racing heroes, endowed their exploits with the simple grandeur and unsullied authenticity for which we long.

Just as cycling lore looked back on a golden age of sure purpose and epic struggle, so it was with the comrades. As communism collapsed all over Eastern Europe and in the Soviet Union itself, even our much-revised and diligently patched Marxism crumbled through our fingers. By the beginning of the 1990s, I found I had belonged unwittingly to the last generation that had been able to cling to this peculiar anachronism, the last generation for whom the communist dream of a system-built better world had still been just barely tenable. Someone once remarked that the party of ex-Communists – the disillusioned who had renounced their membership or simply walked away from it – was the largest party of all. As the original illusion dissolved before us, even disillusion was no longer possible. Instead a vacuum, a poignant emptiness, was bequeathed us.

My last Party card is for 1989. They printed in 1990, even after the Berlin Wall had fallen. While Britain's last few thousand living Communists conducted a desultory debate about what to do with their unwanted franchise, I did not renew my membership.

Cycling became my new home. The small society of racing cyclists offered another noble cause to fill that vacuum, without the ideological baggage. In cycling I found a way to recreate the sense of direction that had abandoned me when the Party softly imploded. But where the communist cause had been about a constant refining of means towards endlessly postponed utopian ends, cycling, with its satisfying circularities, presented itself as an ideal project: one in which the means and ends were identical. I would travel with Fausto Coppi whose slogan was simple: 'Ride a bike, ride a bike, ride a bike.'

It was Mick who found out about a club to join. In the beginning, he was the more committed of the two of us. From the British Cycling Federation he learned that there were several cycling clubs in our area of south-east London: the Dulwich Paragon Cycling Club, the De Laune CC, the Catford Cycling Club, and the Vélo Club de Londres. It was the last of these he picked. The French name appealed to us both. We were ready to be seduced by the romance of life on the wheel.

Especially in southern England, it is not uncommon for British cycling clubs to have the initials VC – VC Etoile, VC Elan, VC Deal. The prefix bears witness to cycle sport's French roots and embodies a sort of internationalism. When it was founded, VC Londres was twinned with VC Le Havre, on the north coast of France. An unofficial exchange programme had taken place, with racers from one club crossing the Channel and staying with members of the other club to take part in races. Mick's instinct served us well in another way, too, for the Vélo Club de Londres (always known as 'VCL' by its members and other club cyclists) had a kind of unofficial residency at the Herne Hill Stadium.

Dating from the turn of the last century, the stadium had become a landmark for London cyclists for decades as the capital's only banked track. The circuit lay tucked discreetly behind a street of large detached houses, a suburban railway line bordering its rear. You might live in that road for years and never know of its existence, only wondering as you tried to park your car why there seemed to be so many cyclists around on summer evenings.

The track was a large oval, approximately 400 metres in

circumference, steeply banked at either end, where the radius of the curve was shortest, but with back and home straights that were almost flat. The home straight carried riders past a modest grandstand and clubhouse, beneath which were the changing rooms.

When Mick and I paid our first visits to Herne Hill, it looked run-down and neglected. Cycling being a minority sport, the Council had neither the money to invest nor the inclination to develop it. The grandstand was shabby and the track itself in need of repair. The tarmac had been ill-laid the last time it was resurfaced; now it was pitted and scarred, especially on the north-facing bank that got the worst of winter frosts.

Yet Herne Hill clung to its former prestige. It still possessed an atmosphere of faded glory, like a once fashionable, now down-at-heel seaside resort. We could only guess at the exploits that these banks and straights had seen. Heroic sprints ending in desperate lunges for the line. Lonely pursuiters belting around and around, their legs a-blur. The chaotic pell-mell of a points race or Madison, full of incident – frantic chases and sometimes bone-jarring crashes. The crowds, cheering not only from the bunting-decked grandstand, but lining the trackside ten-deep, come to see men whose names were legends then – Reg Harris, Tommy Simpson, Hugh Porter – competing against ordinary clubmen – Dave Bonner of the Coulsdon Club and Wally Happy of the Norwood Paragon.

The VCL met every Saturday morning for training. This was a public session, open to anyone, but it had a strong club identity. There was a resident coach, retained on a modest stipend by the local authority. Mike Daley was a slender, unsmiling man who always wore a navy-blue tracksuit. He might have been in his early fifties, he might have been nearer seventy – it was difficult to tell. He never rode a bike, nor spoke of his own cycling days, but the rumour once went round that he still shaved his legs.

Those Saturday morning sessions, when he would stalk the track's inner perimeter with loud-hailer in hand issuing terse instructions, were his possession, his gift. On winter evenings he ran weekly circuit-training sessions in a nearby school gymnasium. Daley pushed us hard, exhorting us through the routine of sit-ups, pull-ups and squat-thrusts in that oddly clipped manner that he had. But a natural reserve made him too mild to be a martinet. He had no small talk, unless it was for cycling, and then he would look off into the middle distance, as though his attention needed always to be on the riders.

You tried hard for Mike Daley because you saw that his devotion to his work was unswerving. Cycling was his life. He would often travel to races across London or out into Kent and Surrey, even if there were only a single VCL rider on the start sheet. In a passive way he was liked, and grudgingly admired, by club members; which was probably fine with him, for it was not his purpose to be loved. But without him, there would have been no VCL.

Daley had a special bond with the club's resident pro, Robert Knight. Knight was a former national sprint champion, a long-time professional, and Daley's protégé since his schooldays as a rising junior talent. They could not have been more different in personality, yet they had developed a curious symbiosis. Rob was a born athlete; you could read it in his physique. In his aura of unshakable self-belief, he was like a south London version of the varsity football hero. Rob was easy and affable, where Daley was awkward and taciturn.

Yet together they made a team. On Saturday mornings Rob would get riders organised out on the track, co-ordinating his instructions with Daley who would stand down by the finishing straight. In effect, Rob acted as Daley's coaching assistant, giving individual advice and guiding novices as he rode while Daley took care of the big picture. In turn, Daley acted as Rob's confidante and unofficial manager.

That first Saturday, as I nervously made my way down the driveway between the houses that led to the track, I was alone. Mick had just taken a job in a cycle shop. He was relieved to get out of couriering, with its relentless graft, the noise and grime of traffic, and the ever-present danger of being knocked off, but the new job meant that he had to work weekends.

Everyone had to ride a track bike. No bike with gears or brakes was permitted. Many of the riders, already now circling the shallow ellipsis of the tarmac bowl, seemed to have their own machines. It was a motley crowd, cyclists of all different shapes, sizes and ages, but a good number wore the blue and red vertical striped jersey of the VCL. I got myself issued with one of the club's ancient stock of track bikes. They were basic in quality, many part-cannibalised to maintain the better models. I picked the most functional one in my size that I could see, borrowing a spanner to raise the saddle to the right height and fiddling with the stiff old leather straps so that the pedal clips would hold my cleated shoes.

Track bikes are always fixed. There is no freewheel mechanism. The only way you can change the ratio of the gear (which by tradition is given as the number of inches the bike will travel for one complete rotation of the pedals) is to take the rear wheel out and swap the cog for another of greater or lesser circumference (measured by the number of teeth). Because of the tool you'd need – a long-armed, heavy implement called a chain whip that grips the cog and unscrews it – this is a job you would generally do in the workshop rather than at the trackside. As long as the bike is moving, the pedals must rotate – your feet with them, willy-nilly. When you are used to a normal road bike, that lets you coast without pedalling, the sensation of riding a track bike is unnerving. It is as if the bike has a will of its own.

I took my borrowed bike out on the track and slowly built up momentum. After a few laps, I tried getting out of the saddle to accelerate, which was fine. Except that, as I sat down again, I did what comes naturally on a road bike, which is to stop pedalling for a moment until one's position in the saddle is comfortably adjusted. The instant I did so, the bike bucked under me, as though trying to throw me off. My legs were pulled violently, almost dislocated at the knee it felt, as they were forced to resume a pedalling motion.

I wobbled, nearly lost it, but learned my lesson. Never, ever stop pedalling on a track bike. You can apply gentle resistance to slow down, using the banking in tandem, but you must always obey the bike's mechanical imperative, its instinctive quest for perpetual motion.

For a beginner, as I was, the concept of a bicycle without any brakes is unnerving and counter-intuitive. Especially on a fixed, where even slowing down is of necessity a gentle, gradual process. Riding a bike without brakes in close formation with other riders was a still scarier prospect. Paradoxically, on the track, cyclists ride even more tightly bunched than on the road.

Most track races are very intense and of only a few minutes duration. This makes your position in the bunch at every moment critical. Just to keep your place, you have to ensure that you leave no gap. If the smallest space opens up between you and the rider in front, another will move up and take the spot. There are times when you have to be ruthless, even physically forceful – riding with your elbows out, prepared to go shoulder to shoulder if someone tries leaning on you. If you are nervous and hesitant about following wheels and guarding your position, before you know it you have ended up on the back of the bunch, which is never the place to be. There are three very good reasons not to be on the back. First, it is the most dangerous place in the bunch: any crash in front of you will very likely bring you down with it. Second, and paradoxically, you often have to work harder at the back than anywhere else because any change of pace at the front is amplified down the line, so that backmarkers find themselves constantly yo-yoing between having to speed up and slow down. And last, when the hammer goes down, you are going to be the first to get dropped.

Riding close is vital, to keep your place and hide from the wind, but it is hard to learn because it involves trust. Every rider has to trust every other not to do something stupid, unpredictable or dangerous. Every rider has to give up some portion of his autonomy for the collective safety of the bunch.

— Move up, move up, shouted Rob from behind at our ragged group. — Close the gaps.

Anxious, feeling at any moment that the rider in front might slow down and send me hurtling into him, I inched gingerly closer to the bike in front, but still leaving a good four or five feet. As the formation tightened up, the gap I was leaving began to show. All of a sudden, Rob was level with me, resting an arm on my shoulder.

— Move up; get in really close. Though not out of breath, he spoke fast. — Your front wheel should be a foot away from his back wheel: twelve inches max. Don't overlap his wheel, but you should be close enough that you can reach forward and touch his arse. All right?

I nodded. And tried to move as close as he was saying. It felt impossible, that even to attempt it would spell instant disaster. Apart from the incident with the taxi and then once as a student, when I braked foolhardily on a frosty morning and fell flat on my face, cutting my chin, I had not come off a bike. I was not keen to repeat the experience. The track surface was gritty and abrasive, and now my feet were tightly strapped into the pedals. Often, I'd been told, riders would be injured not by the fall itself, but because one foot would stay trapped in its clip while the bike twisted away from the fallen cyclist. Clipless pedals, which were based on the technology of ski-bindings and allowed your feet to snap out sideways, were only just coming on the market then.

— That's it, but closer still. Now I felt Rob's hand on my shoulder, encouraging, pushing me forward.

— Don't look at his wheel; look right there. And he reached forward and touched the rider in front just where his shorts met his jersey.

Mike and Rob soon had us in pairs, making two parallel lines just a yard or so apart, circling the track at a steady tempo. Each pair would take a turn on the front for a lap, and then swing off the front up the banking. As the double line of riders passed below them, the pair would use the banking first to decelerate and then, swinging down, to speed up again to rejoin the bunch at the back.

This discipline, called *through and off*, is the foundation of riding in formation. It is the fundamental technique of racing: how a breakaway group organises itself to elude the pack; how, too, the bunch will organise itself to chase down the escape. In this simple technique of shared effort lies the principle of cycle-racing's strange blend of cooperation and competition. The underlying logic of a race – beneath its often bewildering, confused choreography – is determined by the complex system of shifting, temporary alliances that form as some riders combine to escape, others to chase. That mix of mutual aid and ruthless aggression is regulated by an unwritten but elaborate etiquette – in effect, a racer's code of honour.

At that time I had not the faintest apprehension of such a code and its fine nuances. First, it was necessary simply to learn how to ride in tight formation without falling off or, worse, causing someone else to fall off. Even now, others depended on me and my bikecraft. After half an hour of riding round and round, going through and off, varying the pace, Daley called out, 'Next lap: sprint'.

Sprint?! What did this mean? I looked around. At first, nothing happened; everyone stayed in line as we came down the finishing straight once more. But as we hit the curve, several riders who had been placed at the back started to break out of formation and move up the bunch, higher on the banking. As we rounded on to the back straight, the pace started to build. I found myself going faster, sucked along by the gathering momentum of the bunch. Suddenly, the neat order of the formation was gone: riders were moving everywhere, jockeying for position, squeezing into gaps, trying to find a good position to launch their effort without finding themselves prematurely on the front, forced to *lead out* the sprint.

After the tameness of the exercises, the sudden liberty of speed was thrilling. I tried to maintain my place but, still nervous about riding so close and anxious to keep a clear patch of track immediately in front of me, I found myself slipping towards the back of the bunch. As we rounded the last curve and hit the home straight, riders were swooping down off the banking. I looked up and saw Rob, more than fifty metres ahead, flying towards the line with a couple of riders trying to stay with him and challenge the sprint. Most of the riders in front of me were out of the saddle, weight forward, gripping the bar ends, trying to squeeze every last ounce of effort from their legs. Momentarily I forgot my fear and threw myself into this pell-mell dash. For a second or two I lost myself and became an anonymous part of something much larger like a swarm of angry bees or shoal of silver darting fish.

Right in front of me two riders seemed to wobble and veer into each other. Before I could change direction or react at all there was a blur of bodies and riderless bikes rolling and skating on the floor in front of me. There was no way through.

I felt my front wheel hit something hard. Then all I knew was that I was off. There was nothing to be done now: I tried to relax. The world turned upside down. Light and colour blurred and everything went quiet.

Then I landed. The ground jumped up and mugged me, punching me on the back of my head and kicking me on the shoulder and hip. I scrambled to my feet. Already the adrenaline had kicked in, killing the pain but taking away comprehension. There was a scalding sensation from my shoulder but the pain seemed somehow theoretical, as though it were happening to someone else. I found myself fretting instead about my bright new thermal jacket in the Mondrian-imitation of the La Vie Claire team. Bending round, I saw that the jacket was grazed and holed on the back of my left shoulder, which was where it hurt. I noticed that my neck, too, felt stiff.

Hobbling, but mostly because of the cleats on my cycling shoes, I retrieved my bike. It was wrecked: the front wheel comically distorted, the forks pushed back towards the frame. As I dragged it towards the side of the track, the front tyre exploded with a noise like a gunshot. Looking back down the track, I saw the carnage of the crash. Two other riders and their bikes were still grounded. Daley had run over to one who sat, dazed, on the track, his hands clamped to his forehead.

I tried to orient myself, work out what had happened, though my memory felt vague. Somehow, I had been behind those two riders who had collided and fallen off first. I must then have hit one of the fallen riders, or possibly his bike. My momentum must in turn have sent me airborne. To land on my back, I must have performed about two-thirds of a somersault. All I could think, in my shaken, dissociated state, was that it must have looked spectacular, even balletic, in slow motion. But I was lucky not to have landed on my head or face, or to have snapped a collarbone or wrist trying to break my fall.

That was the end of the training session. One of the downed riders had suffered a cut to his head and Daley was worried about possible concussion. He called us all into the changing room under the grandstand. As we filed in, he came over to me.

— What happened? His eyes searched my face for an answer.

— I don't know exactly, I said. There were two riders in front of me. One of them seemed to hit the other and they both came down. I was right behind them . . . There was nowhere for me to go . . .

— Hmm. OK.

He looked at me sceptically. I was the newcomer, the novice. What was more, it was my bike that was furthest down the track. I could see that it looked from the aftermath as though I had fallen in front of the other two, not behind them. In his mind, I could see I was the most likely culprit, the one who had caused the crash. It was not an unreasonable assumption, but I felt outraged, slandered, all the same.

— I think one of them pulled his foot out of the straps in the sprint, said someone else. And, part exonerated at

46

least, I felt incredibly grateful to him. Daley, though, was not convinced.

After that, it was more than a year before I dared to race in a bunch and much longer still before I rode the track again. But bitten I was.

Stage 3

— You're buying a new bike? Ruth raised a quizzical eyebrow.

Not flinching at the sceptical tone, I applied myself with redoubled energy to the task of scouring a pan.

— Er . . . yeah, I replied reluctantly.

— When are you getting it?

— I've got it already, actually . . . Bought it, I mean. I'm picking it up on Saturday.

— What's wrong with your old one?

— Well, nothing . . . But I needed a better frame and stuff.

— *Stuff*?

— Yeah . . . you know, better brakes, and indexed gears.

— *Indexed*? How much is it then?

— About £600 . . . but it's an incredible bargain: worth nearly double that.

— Yeah, incredible. Well, it's your money, I suppose.

This statement made an artificial distinction, because we more or less pooled our earnings as household income. To which Ruth, then editing a film trade magazine, was the greater net contributor. She had seized the moral high ground by stealth.

— The thing is, I could sell my old bike . . . but I thought

48

you might like it instead. It's actually a little on the small side for me, so it should fit you fine.

— So would I like your cast-off? Thanks.

— Well, I *could* sell it if you don't want it. It's still worth a couple of hundred quid.

— I'm not sure I do want it if it doesn't have *indexed* gears.

A smile slipped over her face despite herself.

— No, but let's be real: it's still about a hundred times better than the rustbucket you're riding at the moment.

— Hmm. All right, then . . . but you have to clean it for me. And pump up the tyres. That's part of the deal.

— OK, done.

I let the water run off a plate before placing it in the rack, with the merest flourish.

The Zen of cycle maintenance was not something I could claim ever to have discovered. Cleaning your own well-tended machine is one thing; looking after your girlfriend's cruddy commuting bike is another. After I'd passed my old bike on to Ruth, it was curious how quickly I fell out of love with the bicycle on which I'd once lavished attention. Now that it was no longer the object of my devotion, it ceased to matter almost altogether. Unloved, it became unlovely. When rain had made the chain start to rust I would squirt some oil on it, but in time this just clogged the whole mechanism with a gritty black grease. At length the state of her bike would move me to give it a quick compassionate rinse and relube. So, with something less than perfect good faith, I fulfilled my side of the bargain.

With my own bike, it was different. I kept the brushed alloys of the chainset shining, the anodised surfaces of the rims dusted and gleaming, even the chain so clean that you could make out every silvered link even at a distance. With experience a smooth-running chain is something you can feel and hear as you ride. It makes a palpable difference to the way a bike performs, more even than a pair of alloy wheel rims or a handmade frame. If there was a lull in the action, the only sound you would be aware of in a big, fast-moving bunch of sixty or seventy riders would be the busy buzzing hum of taut chains flying round chainsets and cogs. This pure kinetic music was the white noise of races. Sometimes you didn't hear it at all; at other times it would blot out everything.

An old chain that had stretched so that its links no longer hugged the teeth of the sprockets snugly, or a chain whose bushes were gummed stiff with oil and dirt, would lose the miraculous efficiency it had possessed when new and still buff with the manufacturer's wax. Once fitted, you needed to lubricate the chain a little to loosen up the links. A little, but not too much: excess oil would pick up dust, especially if the roads were wet. Then the spray from your wheels would fire particles of grit into every moving part. In the space of a single morning's ride a gleaming, purring transmission could be reduced to a creaking mess which looked and ran as though it had been greased with a mixture of sand and molasses.

It was one of the trials of being a bikie that after you had returned from a long, hard winter ride – legs aching, back sore, feeling good for nothing but lying on the sofa – you would have to spend an hour or more bent over your beloved but bespattered bicycle. The salt laid down on winter roads also made it imperative to clean up the bike before corrosion could set in on the non-stainless steel and vulnerable alloy surfaces.

All this had a rational basis somewhere: if you didn't do the maintenance, sooner or later your bike would let you down. Then you'd be marooned out in Kent on a cold, damp Sunday morning, twenty miles from the nearest bike shop – which would in any case be closed – and stuck in your highest gear because of snapped cable. But it was not the wear and tear on my machine that truly motivated me. Like everything else, taking care of the bike went with being serious and disciplined about my cycling. The state of your bike was a visible sign of your aspirations. If you hadn't the will to clean your bike, how would you find the will to train hard enough to race? Preparing yourself and preparing your bike were about commitment. The guys who left last week's grit and grime on their bikes just did not have the right attitude.

When you see a professional, everything about him – bike, jersey, shades, shoes, even legs – has a brilliant showroom shine. If you have ever watched a major race from the roadside, you will have seen this gloss on each rider so deep that it forms a demigod-like golden halo around him. Off their bikes, pros are usually small, slight men. With their weight shaved to 70 kilos or less by constant training and careful diet, they resemble dancers, jockeys or boxers. But on their machines they look much larger. The deep mahogany polish of their tanned, attenuated limbs and the exotic coloration of their jerseys and shorts produce a dazzling aura, like the flare of sunlight down the lens of a camera. Even on the dreariest of days they seem to have this look, as though illuminated from inside by an other-worldly energy.

We could never hope to emulate that. Our jerseys would with time go grey from road grime and frequent washing. Our bikes had to last several seasons and their paintwork soon lost its lustre. Mechanics on the pro teams change the chains on their riders' bikes every day. We would change chains once, or maybe twice a season, and only when the infinitessimal stretch of each link under stress had discernibly compromised its working. But I did my best to look the part, because to do otherwise would have been to brand myself a loser before even starting. Turn out your machine as close to mint as possible and psychologically you already had the jump. If you looked good and your machine was immaculate, it registered with others, even subliminally.

And as I learned to race, my relationship with my bike grew into something else. Mile by mile, the cool external objectivity of its gleaming angles and milled surfaces wore off; it came to feel more and more an organic extension of myself. As I changed bikes, and improved the ones I had, I discovered that every bike had its own *feel* – some combination of the frame type, geometry and componentry, that would have an individual character. Just as a tennis player's service action or a golfer's swing gets so grooved that the racket or club simply feels like an extrusion of hand and arm, a good bike will become part of its rider. Over time and miles, you adapt to each other. An intimacy develops. If you have found your perfect partner, it will dance with you when you stand on the pedals.

By the subtle metamorphosis of an action tediously repeated through training, the banal business of riding a bicycle took on a richness of experience that could not have been guessed at, something not merely satisfying but beautiful. In a memoir of growing up in Beverly Hills, Henry Miller recalled the favourite bicycle of his boyhood as his first love. It was an elegant track bike with a sloping top tube that had been made in Chemnitz before the war (appropriately enough for its new owner, this was in what was then called Bohemia, now part of the modern-day Czech Republic). Miller had bought it at the end of a six-day race that took place in Madison Square Gardens, New York.

The Gardens were where circuses came to visit Manhattan and where, among other popular entertainments, professional bicycle races were held on a temporarily erected wooden track. Bets were laid, fortunes won and lost, while cyclists performed improbable feats such as racing for 24 hours on the trot. To this day there is a type of race named a *Madison*, which involves pairs of riders working as teams and alternately taking a fast lap in and then a lap out to rest. At the changeover, one rider must not only tag the other but grasp his teammate's hand and use his momentum to slingshot his partner up to speed. With several pairs working a circuit it is a spectacular form of racing that makes special demands of strength, skill and courage.

Miller was so proud of his track bike that he cleaned and polished it every time he'd been out on it. He drove his mother to distraction with the oily stains he left in their hall: 'Sometimes she would get so incensed that she would say to me, in full sarcasm, "I'm surprised you don't take that thing to bed with you!" And I would retort — "I would if I had a decent room and a big enough bed."'

To Miller that bike became 'an eternal friend'.

In time, I bought my own lightweight racer, the Donohue in red and blue, and realised something of that relationship. I could not bear for it to be dirty. As that bike came to feel more and more like an extension of my body, keeping it clean became a matter of personal hygiene. Though the cleaning and maintenance always remained a chore, the task fell lightly on me. It was always easy to fill a Saturday afternoon that way when there was nothing on TV but the monotonous clacking of the teleprinter telling the football scores. Sitting on the living-room floor with an old towel spread out, I began by stripping down a hub. Once exposed I would wipe clean every one of the dozen ballbearings on each side of the axle. Then I dropped them one by one back into their race, squeezed in a fresh lick of lithium grease and finally reassembled the hub. The last delicate touch of this operation involved locking the cones just tight enough to hold the bearings firmly in place and to keep the rim running true, but not so tight as to interfere with the hub's slick rotation.

It was a methodical task, and one that made a mindless but pleasant way of filling those miraculously empty hours. But at the end of it was something perfectly accomplished. A little nugget of Zen after all.

— Ugh! Get those away from me.

Ruth flinched from me in bed as if I had concealed a pocket-sized cattle-prod under the duvet.

— They're scratchy!

— No they're not, I retorted.

It had been three days now since I first shaved my legs. Reaching down I could feel that there was the beginning of stubble. To me, though, it seemed quite gentle, not bristly like an actual beard.

— Look, really, *feel*. It's soft, not scratchy. I went on in my most emollient tone. I moved my legs back towards hers.

— Don't! she shrieked. It *is* scratchy.

She gathered up the duvet to tuck under her legs, barring further contact, and buried her nose in the new issue of *Vogue*.

I switched off the light on my side. After lying on my back for a minute, listening to our breathing slowing and synchronising, I moved in closer. A brief pas-de-deux took place beneath the duvet. Eventually, we found a way of sleeping together, my belly warming her lumbar region, but my legs pulled back and hers drawn up so as not to touch.

The hardest part was the knees: all craggy outcrops and shadowy depressions at the front which the careless razor would try to carve into smooth contours like some evil miniature earthmover. And at the back were all those awkward creases and vulnerable tendons. It was a delicate business in many respects.

Seeing my legs shaved for the first time, pink from the bath and suddenly smooth, was unnerving. It was as if they belonged to someone else. They didn't look like a woman's legs, yet they didn't look like a man's either. They seemed more muscular than mine, and at the same time more slender. They had something of the faintly uncanny androgyny of a dancer's legs.

Shaving is so little spoken of, yet something that unites all racing cyclists. I thought of the riders of the Tour. This had to be something they too experienced, I reflected, unless perhaps their legs were shaved for them by the *soigneur* – a role that was part bottle-washer, part physical therapist, and part spiritual adviser.

For cyclists, the real question of shaving, the one which no one dares to ask, is where to stop. In changing rooms at race controls you would see all sorts of ad hoc solutions to this conundrum. Some would shave to just above the point which their Lycra shorts would reach. This was fine as far as it went, you might say, but in the changing room it looked ridiculous because it created the distinct visual impression that they were wearing a pair of hair shorts. On a particularly hirsuit cyclist it could look like a pair of opaque tights cut off above the knee. Others would shave higher, but the one thing a cyclist could not do was shave right up to his 'bikini line'. The effect of friction from the Lycra shorts' chamois insert on inner thigh stubble was not to be contemplated.

Eventually I found a compromise I was happy with, shaving all the way to the top of my thigh on the outside of my leg, but leaving something near the top of my inside leg. The ritual of shaving became a comfortable part of my Saturday night routine so that my legs would be smooth and pristine for the Sunday race. With practice I had it down to about 15 or 20 minutes, not much longer than I would have spent in the bath in any case.

Getting into bed, at least, was a beatific experience. The feel of the sheets, cool and unmediated, was a caress, a sensation akin to entering water. Jumping into a swimming pool with shaved legs also now had a shockingly new sensual directness. It was like a melody, familiar from listening to a crackly old analogue recording, now heard with the crisp digital clarity of a CD.

I was self-conscious about wearing ordinary shorts off the bike. This was not only because my legs were shaved, but also because of the strange tan-line caused by wearing cycle shorts. If you were going to wear ordinary shorts, you had to find ones that reached the knee, otherwise you would expose a ridiculous white ring of underexposed thigh. Among civilians I may have been embarrassed by my shaved legs, but at the same time I was flattered when someone noticed. It gave me a chance to proclaim that I was a cyclist; not just a cyclist, but a *racing* cyclist. To shave your legs, I felt, was to claim and wear the badge of membership to a select fraternity. It was like someone noticing the party card in your wallet. It made me proud.

A select, but not exclusive, band. Shaving is common among bodybuilders and swimmers who shave not only their legs, but their whole body. For swimmers, there is an obvious hydrodynamic effect: hairs trap air bubbles close to the skin and cause drag. Compared with air, water is a thousand times more viscous: any source of drag that can be eliminated is potentially significant in a race that might be decided by hundredths of a second. Swimmers also speak of the enhanced *feel* for the water that shaving down gives them. In preparation for the Seoul Olympics Matt Biondi's coach had him swim with dolphins to develop an empathy with their effortless propulsion. Swimmers talk about *catching the water* with their stroke as though by stealth. They learn to feel, rather than force, a way through the water. Besides speed, strength and stamina, swimmers seem to need that intimacy with their element.

Cyclists do not have the same relationship with the air through which they move. Not that aerodynamics are insignificant: above 20mph, virtually all the work a cyclist does is in maintaining his speed against the air resistance offered by his body and his bike. It is enough to ride into the wind to discover how much difference this means. Nothing is more soul-destroying than constantly toiling against a heavy headwind that reduces you to an arduous crawl in a low gear. It feels like trudging up an endless incline, but with the psychologically crushing knowledge that you are riding on the flat.

The benefit of shaved legs is negligible in this situation, even though the popular assumption persists that cyclists shave their legs mainly for aerodynamic effect. Except possibly for a small number of specialised track-racing events, like the Olympic sprint (a one-kilometre dash against the clock), this is not the case. In road-racing there are too many variables that are much more significant.

But since the explanations from cyclists themselves about why they shave their legs vary so widely, a degree of general confusion seems understandable. Some riders maintain that shaving makes the cleaning and dressing of wounds easier. If you fall at 30mph the blacktop takes off your skin like emery paper set in concrete. Crashes, or *chutes* as the French call them, are an occupational hazard of racing. You are not permitted to hold a racing licence without proving that you are up to date with your tetanus jabs. Some riders are good at avoiding spills; others seem so accident prone as to be jinxed. Experience helps. I crashed out of races all too often in my first two seasons, and had to learn to live with those abrasions known in the trade as *road rash*. It can be hard to sleep, you discover, when it is impossible to lie on one side because of the raw skin on top and the deep bruise beneath. Sometimes the abrasion would suppurate for days into its gauze bandage before it finally dried and began to heal. Perhaps it was my imagination, but in those days I would sometimes feel a powerful thirst as though my body were losing fluid like a burns victim's.

According to this 'clean wound' theory of shaving, smooth legs are less susceptible to going septic in the event of a scrape. But hair or no, saline solution from an aerosol made an effective cleanser. And because the wound takes several weeks to heal completely, the hairs would grow back in the meantime regardless. Then again, if the graze were severe enough, you might well get treatment with antibiotic powder as well. I was never convinced by the theory. I still have the scars on my hips, flanks and elbows to back me up.

Another rationale for shaving is that many riders like to use warm-up balm on their legs, especially before races in the early season when the weather is often still cold and wet. The idea is that the embrocation helps get the circulation going and heats up cold muscles. At least it's true that your legs feel partly anaesthetised by the orange mentholated goo sold by specialist bikeshops. The logic of shaving here is that to rub in embrocation through hairy legs would be a messy task, and to clean up after a race would be even more thankless. After three or four hours on wet roads, all kinds of muck will have adhered to your shins, all the more so if they were earlier coated with the greasy jelly of the warm-up balm.

The embrocation argument carries marginally more weight than the others. In the early season almost everyone would use the stuff. It was part of the ritual of preparation for the race. You had only to enter a shabby village hall on a chilly Sunday morning in March and the eye-watering aroma of embrocation would assault your nostrils with its potent medicinal blast. It was as though someone had been using a huge tub of Vick as floor polish. That menthol smell was as integral to the atmosphere of the changing room as the racers' stilted conversation, forced laughter and tense silences. Even more than the stink from the outside latrines as one rider after another queued up to evacuate their bowels, embrocation was synonymous with pre-race nerves.

The real reason cyclists shave their legs is very simple: it is because everyone else does it. No one likes to make a direct admission of the fact but, secretly for all, shaving one's legs has above all an aesthetic dimension: it is simply how the racing cyclist should look.

When you shave your legs for the first time, then, you undergo a self-administered rite of initiation. More than anything else you might have done up to that point, it means that you have decided to become a racing cyclist. You have joined the club. And because everyone who races, almost without exception and regardless of level and ability, does shave their legs, hairy legs in cycle shorts soon come to appear gross and ludicrous. Only someone who is willing to look like a rank novice, a complete outsider or an utter loser, would turn up to race with hairy legs.

Very often what is aesthetic in cycling also has a more concrete purpose. When you are riding in the bunch, you are always following wheels. It is only natural to register what the legs of the guy in front look like – how defined, for instance, the muscles of his calves are. Subconsciously, you assess them for what they may tell you about how fit and strong that rider might be. There it is, written out in front of you, just from seeing the backs of his shaven legs. If they look *cut* or *ripped*, in those expressions which cyclists sometimes borrow from bodybuilding, it is an indication of how low his body fat is. It means he's been training hard. If his muscles are massive and heavy, however, you can bet that this rider has a strong sprint but will struggle when the road goes uphill.

In a race it is all information. It doesn't tell you everything, and there are many more explicit ways of reading a race and judging which riders will just want to follow wheels and who will really be willing to work. Still you watch, you see who has the legs, as they say. Another of cycling's compulsions, its secret knowledge, it becomes second nature.

Off his bike, Andy was a saxophonist. He had been on the scene. For a time, in the mid-eighties, he had been close to making it big with a band that had a couple of chart hits. And for a time, he used to hint, he had enjoyed the lifestyle – the gigs and the groupies. Now he had a steady girlfriend and he played jazz. He would do weddings and pub gigs for cash, and ran his own quartet for kicks, but he had ambitions for the jazz-funk outfit he fronted. They were hoping to sign a recording contract. When I first knew him, it seemed that the saxophone and the bicycle vied equally for his time.

Being self-employed and having, besides, irregular hours of employment, Andy was often available for a training ride when I could get an afternoon off. Whereas Mick's job at the Mosquito Bikes retail and repair co-op was bounded by shop hours. Mosquito was one of the last surviving ventures from the crop of cooperatives in London that had been seeded by the counterculture of the seventies. Progressive in design values as well as politics, it used to advertise stylishly in *Marxism Today*. But by the early nineties, 'MT' had gone and even the final remnant of the underground press, *City*

Limits, was in decline. Mosquito moved with the times and restructured its ownership to give its permanent employees a genuine stake, abandoning the old cooperative status. But it retained some of the old ethos, and by virtue of its position on the Essex Road, did good business with the liberal lawyers, lefty journalists and sundry commuters who pedalled down from Islington and Stoke Newington. Although his patience would often be tried by these nonconformist folk who, despite their principles and paid-up union memberships, seemed surprised that a co-op should charge for labour at all, Mick had found his natural home.

Andy also belonged to the VCL and, when we started riding together, had already raced with Mick for a season. Spooked by my first session at the track that had ended in a crash, I put off racing for another year. Then, the first time out at a race near Reigate that Mick had talked me into entering, I found myself slipping to the back before the race had even started. The neutralised zone included a steep, twisting descent. Wary of the tricky-looking cambers, I kept feathering the brakes the whole way down. Before I knew it, riders were flying by me on both sides with what seemed suicidal recklessness.

Neutralised zones are a feature of most road races, which begin with a rolling start. They are necessary because the race HQ does not usually sit on the racing circuit itself, so the zone can extend to anything from a few hundred yards to a couple of miles – whatever it takes to reach the recognised circuit. The term 'neutralised' is misleading: officially, no racing is permitted until the commissaire's flag in the lead car goes down; in practice, the jostling for position can be fierce and uncompromising. Unprepared for this, and totally intimidated by the idea of riding at speed in such a large bunch of cyclists, I was already right at the back of the peloton when the race got under way. (We never used the word 'peloton', in fact, except when talking about the Tour; it would have been an affectation. We belonged 'in the bunch'.) Soon I was struggling to stay in touch, and then, with scarcely a mile gone, there was a contact of wheels and a crash among the riders at the rear. I skidded to a stop behind the mêlée of fallen cyclists, my worst fears brought to life right in front of me – only, miraculously, this time I had escaped injury myself. Is there a crash every time they go out? I remember thinking. Who would go in for this sort of craziness?

By the time I had recovered my composure and got my feet back in the straps, the bunch was half a mile down the road. I chased forlornly with a handful of others for half a circuit until, winded and dispirited, I decided to 'pack', as they say, and soft-pedalled back to the HQ. Mick soon joined me there. He'd survived the crash, but after another lap the pace had proved too high and he had been dropped. Cycle-racing, I concluded, is a sport for the stupidly fearless and the super-tough. I skipped the idea of racing for the rest of that season, too.

But Mick was less easily discouraged, and he was soon finishing races and then collecting his first points for getting placed. I felt inadequate and envious as my friend and cycling companion had moved into a different league. Though we belonged to the same club, he had been initiated into something higher, whose rites I could only guess at. For a time it seemed as though we were now set on different paths, and I envied him, too, for the bond he had formed with Andy. They raced as a pair, looking out for each other, working as allies in breaks, or one protecting the other's advantage by acting as 'policeman' of the group that was away.

But I did not entirely lack Mick's drive to compete, and I worked hard at my fitness. I was always ready to go out training, and so Andy and I, loafers both, would often ride out together on a weekday afternoon. Hard rides he took me on, along lanes on the Downs and through the Weald that were still new to me. He was race-fit, so I had to work to hold his wheel on the climbs. Always on the last long drag home up to Crystal Palace, though, he'd murder me. He would wind up the pace slowly in a big gear until I just couldn't hold his wheel. Then there he'd be, waiting at the top, looking as fresh as he had sixty or seventy miles earlier, as I heaved myself up the last few yards of gradient, panting, weak, and ready to vomit.

Andy used to ride a Dutch-made bike, resprayed blue, with an ancient Campag groupset, and a worn, dark-blue leather saddle with 'turbo' spelt across the back. I spent hours following his wheel vacantly reading that logo. I can still see it, as though the image were tattooed on my retina. When it came to kit, Andy was old-school. If they had still been available, he might have preferred the old woollen shorts. On warm days he used to ride with his Lycra shorts rolled back anyway, so that they were shorter on the leg. He used to say that it was to get more of a tan, but it made him look as though he were wearing woollens.

He made no concessions to the yearly shifting fashions of pro team jerseys with their debased collages of sponsors' logos, or to the gaudily day-glo creations of sensibly attired commuting cyclists. Unless he was racing, when he had to wear a club jersey, Andy would always wear plain black. It gave him the look of a time-triallist from the fifties who, in those days, used to wear jackets knitted from black alpaca wool. In presence and appearance, Andy faintly resembled Britain's postwar track-cycling hero, Reg Harris. He had the same forthright, pugnacious attitude, the same stocky physique and powerful thighs.

— So what happened? I asked on a ride one day, provoked by a nonchalant allusion to his glamorous past in the band.

— Oh, the usual. A few singles that did all right, a tour as supporting band that looked promising . . . but then the album didn't do so well, and there'd start to be arguments backstage. The record company, *of course*, was crap and wouldn't renew our contract. Suddenly there's no money coming in and someone gets a better offer . . . and so the band splits up.

— Don't you miss it? I asked.

— Nah. You do it once and either you make it and then it's your career, or you outgrow it.

— So what now?

— Practise the saxophone. Ride my bike. And maybe do teacher training.

Andy always knew where he was in the world and where he was going. He had an old-fashioned integrity and a brick-like self-confidence which I at once admired and coveted. It was as though doubt and angst were just not part of his repertoire.

So when I started racing again, it was Andy who took me under his wing. Mick had already graduated, and now I was the novice clubmate to whom he could teach a thing or two. Not that he was a spectacularly successful racer himself, but he knew how to race, and he was a slogger. As for me, the club runs and summer evening training rides, which sometimes involved groups of a dozen or more riders, had gradually accustomed me to riding hard and fast in close formation. I was still very green but along the way I had shed some of my fear.

Although Andy looked heavy for a cyclist, with footballer's thighs, he regularly won the club hill climb. Over a short steep incline he had tremendous power and speed, able to push an improbable gear, the frame of his bike almost visibly flexing under the load. And he knew how to hurt himself too; how to stay with the pain and overcome it. They used to say, the old boys you'd sometimes ride beside on a club run, that in the early days the men who became professional racing cyclists were often farmers' sons, accustomed to back-breaking work, used to toiling away no matter the weather. Andy was hardly from peasant stock – his family came from Liverpool (and this I know because he once rode from London to Liverpool in a day to visit them) – but in that willingness to battle on, which I later came to recognise as the mark of any racer worthy of respect, he had something of that old nobility.

Considering his build, he had good stamina, but his places in long races came hard won. He was a cautious racer, and an unorthodox one – preferring to sit right at the back of the bunch and survey affairs from there. Andy often acted as the self-appointed *patron*, the boss of the bunch. If he thought someone was riding like an idiot, he would tell them. And they'd know they'd been told. Some might have resented his assumption of command, but most were tacitly grateful. A race where everyone is at sixes and sevens, constantly attacking and counter-attacking to no effect, soon becomes frustrating; sometimes you want someone to take charge and organise affairs. Bernard Hinault, five times Tour winner, was famous for deciding how any given day's racing was to be run, and few riders were willing to provoke his displeasure for fear of being worked over by him and his lieutenants – forced to chase a concerted attack, and spat out the back at the slightest hint of vulnerability. There was something of 'the Badger', as the French knew Hinault, about Andy and he revelled in the role, largely symbolic though it was.

There was an early race, a 'pipe-opener' it was called, that we did together one soggy Sunday morning in the rolling countryside of Kent, south of the Weald. I had worked hard all winter for this, my first full season of racing, and was all keenness. The bunch set off at an easy lick, barely working enough to break a sweat in the damp March air. After just a few miles I lost patience and launched an attack. I was dangling off the front just a few hundred yards up the road for most of the first lap; no one bothered to join me. It was exhilarating to escape so easily, but also unnerving – what now? Over the next few miles, the gap stabilised at about two hundred yards. Riding on your own, I was discovering, is much harder work than sitting in the bunch following wheels.

Going away on the first lap, I had seen nothing of the circuit. Now, as we reached the main climb, I was starting to suffer. I looked back, and the gap was closing fast. In another instant the bunch came by me at what seemed an impossible pace. I realised later that someone had chosen to put in an attack on the climb – a classic tactic because the hills are where the valuable few seconds are made that turn into unbridgeable gaps once back on the flat – and the bunch was responding to this serious move. Before I knew it, Andy came by me, barking at me to pick up the pace and get back in the bunch. I knew it was serious because he always rode as practically the backmarker. I just managed to keep contact, and was rewarded by a succinct lecture on not riding like a fool.

I hung on for another lap, but when the same thing happened the next time up the climb I just couldn't keep pace. It was much, much harder than anything I had encountered on the weekly club runs. In racing it seemed a whole other level of performance was demanded. In a matter of seconds, I slipped backwards through the bunch and then, suddenly, there was no one left around me. Before I could even taste the disappointment and ignominy, I was *out the back*. I lurched out of the saddle one more time and tried to spur my bike on, but my legs were in pieces. I had been dropped.

I chased for another lap, along with a pair of vets, two guys old enough to be my dad. As the morning mist turned to chilly rain, the road became greasy. I felt my back wheel slip sideways fractionally on a fast curve, and began to lose my nerve. In the end, I couldn't even hold the wheels of the two vets. Wet and sorry, I climbed off as the circuit passed the turn-off to the HQ.

Andy more often followed wheels than made moves, but he also had legs and a bottomless fund of determination. The rain came down, the laps went on; more and more bedraggled riders packed. As the bunch whittled down, Andy ended up in the lead group on the road, about nine or ten riders left in contention. Putting on a rain cape, I went back to see the end of the race, which finished at the top of the long drag which had been my nemesis. The leaders came in: the first few, in twos or threes, sprinting desperately elbow-to-elbow for the places, but the runners-up came over one by one. Gasping, sag-shouldered, grateful merely to get to the line.

Finally Andy arrived bringing up the rear, looking shattered, in ninth place. He climbed off his bike, and stood stiffly doubled over, trying to catch his breath. I offered some mumbled congratulation, but when he straightened, I could see that he was furious.

— That cunt came past me! That slippery little shit! I'm going to have words with him. He can't do that.

With that he got back on his bike, and set off grim-faced towards the changing room in the diminutive village hall. I had no idea what he was on about, although it was clear some foul play had been involved.

— What happened? I asked, catching up with him and watching his face in profile.

— That guy in the Central Sussex, he was completely fucked for the last lap. Never did a turn. We could have got rid of him, but I got things organised in the break and I told him he could sit on the back as long as he didn't try to come round anyone at the end. Then he did, he came round me, the bastard! You just can't do that. He's gonna learn.

I was nervous then. Andy had once decked someone after a race, after a prolonged and heated debate in the saddle which continued in the changing room. One punch and the argument was settled.

Andy stowed his bike among the others leaning against the mossy Edwardian brickwork of the hall. With so many non-finishers changed and departed, the place was already half empty. He marched as purposefully as his cleated shoes allowed into the dim, musty hall. His adversary was sitting on a bench with his shoes and socks off, but otherwise still in his kit — including the team jersey which identified him as the offender. His gangling legs were luminously white where he'd succeeded in scrubbing off the road grime.

He was much younger, and lighter, than Andy. This was a relief: he didn't look as though he'd be likely to get up and start trading blows.

— That was fucking *outrageous*, bellowed Andy, standing right over him so close that if the kid had tried to stand up they'd have been eyeball to eyeball. — You did no work but we let you sit in. You weren't going to contest the points. That was the deal.

Glancing up at Andy, the guy looked very young and very small. Either to save face, or simply because he didn't know what else to do with himself, he made a show of carrying on cleaning his shins.

— I never agreed to nothing. It was you said that. It came out as a whine. No one was taking his side.

— You agreed and you fucking know it, Andy went on. —

We could have dropped you anytime. When we let you sit in, it was understood that you were getting a free ride but you weren't in the race any longer. As far as I'm concerned, you gave me your word and you broke it. You just *don't* do that. Andy let that last sentence sink in, before breaking away and stalking back to where his bag lay on a plastic bucket seat next to me.

— Yeah, sorry, OK? . . . Sorry, mate.

— Well, don't do it again. Andy's anger was subsiding, but as if he were geared for confrontation and did not know how to respond to the lad's abject apology and penitential posture, it momentarily sparked into life again. — You just don't do that *in a race!*

On the way home in the car, conversation between Andy and me was stilted. He seemed angry still, and I felt oddly implicated in the offender's guilt. Perhaps I knew that I could easily have made the same mistake. Would I have known better? It seemed so arcane and weird, this chivalric code that overruled the goal of winning and required a man's word to be his bond on pain of losing his honour.

It dawned on me that Andy knew his vocation as a teacher after all. He had a natural authority; no one would dare mess around at the back of his classes. He would be the sort of tough-but-fair teacher who, as a kid, you would have looked up to and striven to please because you'd have wanted his approval more than anything in the world. He would command respect because he possessed a notion of decency, loyalty and fair play, and a sense of comradeship and its responsibilities. And he believed in these passionately enough to be willing to enforce them, even to fight for them. These values seemed to stem from cycling, as though that were their source, and spread to the rest of his life. I took the lesson.

* * *

— Don't you want to come and hear Andy play at The Kerfield? I asked.

— Where's that? Ruth replied, stalling, still reading the paper.

— Off Camberwell Grove, I think.

— When?

— Tomorrow night. I *did* tell you about it.

Ruth reached for her bag, pulled out her filofax and flipped it open. She would neatly clip the corner off each week that had passed, so that her diary always fell open where her finger stopped it, at the current week. She was like that, meticulous in certain things.

— Nah, can't. Got a film screening to go to.

— What is it?

— I can't remember. Probably some Hollywood trash.

— So why not skip it and come and hear Andy?

Ruth sighed, closing the ring-bound diary and pressing down the popper on its low-grade leather skin. The gesture made her decision final. I felt something tighten in my stomach. Almost like nerves before a race.

— Look, I just don't want to spend two hours in a noisy, smoky pub shouting in someone's ear over the too-loud music, OK?

— It's not going to be too loud. He plays jazz. It's a jazz quartet.

— It's going to be you and your cycling mates, isn't it? So why do you need me there?

— Because . . . I don't know. I'd like you to come. And you might enjoy it.

— Look. With my friends we talk about movies, clothes, TV, music, celebrities, politics, popular culture, whatever. With your friends, you talk about cycling, right?

This was fundamentally correct, but felt unjust all the same.

— So what you're saying is: they're stupid and boring?

— Yes, she said. — OK, not stupid and boring. But they're just *your* friends. It's your world. And that's fine, but I don't have to belong to it ... So *you* go.

Even with Andy's unofficial tuition, it took me a long time to learn how to race, even to the point where I could finish one. The very fact that I was by then fitter than I had ever been seemed almost to delay my development. It made me overestimate my powers. Hotheadedly, I would be in all the action from the off, as though the race would be decided in the first lap. I would try to be in every move, while others saved their legs. Just at the moment when the significant business was being done, when the real *selection* was being made, I would be catching my breath at the back of the bunch. Tactically I was naïve. I was beginning to get the legs to race with, but did not yet have the head for it.

This was a pattern which I later saw repeated in younger clubmates. They would be third cats without a point on their licence, but you knew from the way they could ride that they could be first cats in a single season — if only they learnt how to race. More experienced riders were only too grateful to see these rookies draw the sting from their rivals. They would sit in the bunch while a few worked hard at the front to chase down an early break of young pretenders. As soon as the main bunch made contact again, gathering up the dispirited rump of the riders in the break, that would be their moment to go on the attack. This was the classic tactic of the would-be escapee: attack when your opponents are weary and off-guard, attack at the moment when they are weakest and have least will to respond. Race when no one else wants to race.

Time and again, I would be caught out by this. Only gradually did I learn that the way to race was to ride along inconspicuously, watching, waiting, saying to myself 'Bide your time, bide your time'. It was a matter of patience and a question of observation. You looked out for who was riding strongly, and you recognised the riders whom you had seen before at the head of affairs. You remembered to eat and drink, and you watched and waited. And when they went, you went. It was all timing.

I discovered that you did not even need to be the strongest rider in a race to get placed. You just had to know when to put in a big effort to best effect.

For weeks I showed up at race after race, the blank racing licence in my jersey's back pocket weighing on my mind like the shame of unwanted virginity. At last, success came at Eastway.

A wind-blasted cycle circuit built on the Hackney Marshes, Eastway was named after the strip of two-lane highway that bissected the flat, soggy football fields to the north and the post-industrial wasteland and stockyards of Stratford to the south. The A102(M), the Eastway itself, reared up briefly on pilotis to clamber over the murky River Lea, but any impression of the Westway's iconic, utopian sky-borne highway fell away sharply with the realisation that this was nothing more than a mile-long stretch of dual carriageway linking Hackney to Leytonstone.

A weird oasis in this bleak prospect, Eastway Cycle Circuit possessed a clubhouse with changing rooms and office, which in turn served a campsite to one side. We used to shake our heads in disbelief at the French and Dutch accents we would occasionally hear in the washrooms: who in their right mind would come *here* to camp, at this dismal outpost on Hackney Marshes? But for London's cycle-racing scene, it was an important venue. The races were always well attended and the clubhouse afforded shelter and refreshment, which encouraged more spectators than usually attended bike races. The one-mile distance meant that the riders would lap nearly every two minutes, and there were glimpses of the bunch at other points on the undulating, irregular circuit.

Even so, I was always mindful of how unpromising a spectator sport cycling generally is. Televised racing has expensively solved the problem by equipping a fleet of motorbikes with pillion-riding cameramen to feed back pictures from in among the action via a helicopter link. But spectating an amateur road-race is hardly a pulse-quickening experience. Not surprisingly, before coverage of the Tour de France became a regular annual fixture in the UK, cycle-sport on TV was limited to very occasional forays into track-racing. Until Channel 4's Tour broadcasts in the late eighties, you would be more likely to find greyhound-racing or speedway on TV than cycle racing.

Since I had yet to get any points on my card, I was still racing in 3/J events, so called because they were open to thirds and juniors only. Junior status simply applied to any rider under eighteen at the beginning of the season. Thirds referred to category status: it meant you were a senior rider in the lowest category of three. Everyone began as a *third cat*. You became a *second cat* by winning points – under the system then operating, 15 points. Win another 30 points on top of that in the same season, and you would become a *first cat*. First cat was the highest amateur status, usually entitling you to enter the main professional events in the racing calendar.

To win points, and change category status, you had to be *placed* in a race officially run under British Cycling Federation rules. For a 20-lap race at Eastway, you could only be placed first, second or third, with the points being allotted in descending order 3, 2, 1. For a 60-mile race, one of the Surrey League series, say, there would be places and points for the first six; and for an 80-mile race, there would typically be places down to tenth, with a higher point premium of 15 for the winner, 12 for the runner-up and so on. The longer the race, the more places and points at stake.

Details of all road races were contained in the BCF handbook. Provided you had previously sent a cheque along with the fee for your racing licence to the BCF, this, the racing cyclist's bible, would land on your doormat every year in January, in time for the season's first races in February. Then, when you had pored for hours over the pages and pages of race listings for the whole country with a nervous excitement welling in your stomach and quickening pulse, a foretaste of the pre-race surge of adrenaline, and when you had ringed all the races in which you had an interest and visualised the circuits to which they referred, you had to enter. This required you to fill in a skinny A4 form with name, BCF licence number and club membership, club colours and category status, race for which entered and last three best placings, sign the waiver and mail with appropriate fee (anything from £5 to £10) to the race organiser, whose details were published in the handbook. And then you had to make a cross-referenced note in your diary of all the races you had entered. Mick was always much more efficient at these things than I and he supplied me with the only sheath of these forms I ever needed. When we had first met, he had been social secretary of his local Labour Party branch; I was often reminded why afterwards. He possessed an organisational genius that I did not.

I was someone who had never really got beyond an adolescent resentment of all form-filling as a bureaucratic trespass on my personal autonomy and right to waste time as I saw fit. This arrested development may have had something to do with the fact that my father was methodical in such matters almost to a fault. Perhaps, who knows, my revolt against punctiliousness, my elevation of being flakey to political statement, had an Oedipal character? If this was the case, it was peculiarly self-defeating: there was not much triumph to be had in a life harassed by final demands; still I always waited until the red notice before paying a bill simply because it seemed too tedious and taxing actually to have to find my dog-eared cheque-book and a working biro and fill in the giro slip and write the cheque and steal a stamp from Ruth because I never had any and post the damn thing. For this person then, the protocols of entering a race held under BCF rules were a serious re-education. From that unexpected quarter I finally learned that, given the motivation, there was actually a sense of accomplishment and virtue to be gained by timely, efficient form-filling.

Racing at Eastway ran throughout the summer as a twice-weekly league. The first- and second-cat races were hard-fought over 32 laps, daylight permitting. They were usually dominated by a small number of riders who specialised in sprint finishes and had teams who would work for them to control the races. On the open circuit with two long straights, it was extremely difficult to gain a wide enough gap between a break and the bunch so that the chasers would lose sight of their quarry. Racing is so psychological, even at a collective level, that out of sight is as good as out of mind. On a twisty road circuit through country lanes, a rider can be out of view and forgotten in seconds and half the bunch probably will not even realise that someone has slipped away. But at Eastway it was easy to look over to another part of the circuit and catch sight of any escapees, and for the senior teams this made races easy to control. Generally, you did not expect to win points at Eastway; you went for the workout.

Thirds' and juniors' races were less predictable, more open-ended. It was the lowest category, so abilities would be more mixed. Some of the juniors might be very handy, but if the pace was high they could be at a technical disadvantage. A rule decreed that juniors could not ride a bike with as high a top gear as seniors: the received wisdom was that their still-growing limbs and joints might be damaged by trying to push too big a gear. It meant that on the long downhill straight they could be *spinning out*, unable to pedal fast enough to get any more power out.

More importantly, there was no team control of the 3/J races. They were completely anarchic, in fact. Juniors had the deserved reputation for chasing every move maniacally, yet without being willing to risk the sustained effort that it took to make a break. This made for a jumpy, uneven style of racing, and it could be acutely annoying for riders like me whose best chance of a result would be in a small breakaway. The 3/J races, run over shorter distances, also often ended in bunch sprints – chaotic, pell-mell dashes for the line.

One evening in early May, though, I finally made the right move. It was early in the race for a break, after only eight laps, but with only 12 more to complete, that meant being away for little more than half-an-hour. There was one short climb in the circuit. Its severity required only shifting up a couple of gears, but it was still enough to serve as a launch pad for an attack more often than any other point in the circuit. My attempt was premeditated – there were a couple of riders 200m ahead of us who had already been away for a lap or so, and I planned on joining them. I spent the previous lap carefully positioning myself to make a clean getaway, moving up the bunch but not too near the front to signal my intentions.

Just before the road levelled off I launched myself, sprinting hard for a hundred metres before settling back in the saddle and quickly shifting down a couple of gears. Within seconds my breathing was labouring hard, my heart pounding from the sudden extreme effort. On the downhill straight, I allowed myself a quick look back. I was rewarded with a beautiful view of empty road and just one rider following. Perfect, I had a decent gap.

I put my head down again and made myself as small as I could into the wind as I renewed my pedalling effort. Even in my biggest gear, I tried to concentrate on feeling my legs spin, to keep the pedalling stroke fluid – as if that could fool my body that it wasn't having to hurt.

I was gaining ground rapidly on the two riders ahead. This boosted my morale in one way, but it also implied that they weren't going fast enough. By the time the road started going up again, at the same point where I'd jumped the lap before, I made contact. I was breathing hard, the saliva thickening in my mouth, but I felt good. I rode straight past them, barking hoarsely, 'Come on, let's go', hoping they'd pick up the pace. They looked like juniors, I saw, and my heart sank a little. It meant I couldn't necessarily count on them to work cohesively.

I took them down the straight to give them a chance to recover, and then swung off. Good, they were coming through. At least they knew what to do. As I swung in line behind them, I looked back. The one other rider was gaining on us, but we still had a good gap to the bunch. There'd been no real reaction. It was copybook, almost too easy. I felt magnificent, as though I had evolved, by some strange and stealthy metamorphosis, into a real racer at last.

Soon the other rider joined us. Like me he was older, a third cat. He sat on the back for half a lap, while we continued to take turns. When you've bridged a gap, it is understood in a break that you're allowed brief respite before you have to start pulling your weight. When he came through, we all worked in turn. Four is a perfect number for *through-and-off*. With more riders, it's hard to keep the fluency, and the bigger the group the more likely that its tactical cooperation will break down. But with fewer, just two or three riders, it never feels as though you're getting a rest between turns.

The laps ticked slowly by and the gap back to the bunch seemed to stay safely constant at about two minutes. I kept up a stream of encouragement, but the juniors were tiring. Whenever it was their turn, the pace dipped, and one of us two seniors would have to pull through impatiently. With two laps to go, I lost patience with the truce which had governed our mutual effort. I was still feeling good. In fact, I felt supremely strong, in a way I'd never felt before: as though a powerful breeze were pushing me along, making everything easy. My mind was clear, instead of fuddled by pain and the wish for it to end. I had time to think: we still had a good gap and I knew I couldn't do worse than fourth, but I began to realise, to believe, that I could *win* this.

But fourth would be out of the points. After all this effort, I thought, I have to make this count. When it was my turn to come to the front, I didn't sprint but just poured on the power. I did a long hard turn. The two juniors were so blown already that it was enough to get rid of them.

I looked round and saw my fellow third cat on my wheel. He met my glance and just said, 'Go! Go!' I obeyed, and tore up the back straight, until I figured that it had to be his turn. I was still green, but I did know that you don't want to be in front when it comes to the sprint. The classic tactic is to manoeuvre your opponent, or opponents, into *leading out*. You follow, tucked in to the slipstream, and, as they fade, you come round to deliver the *coup de grâce* with a final burst of speed.

That is the theory. Instead I allowed myself to come through to the front once again just before the road turned the last corner. The tight uphill bend makes you start the final sprint 200m up a slight incline from almost a standing start. I resigned myself to leading out the sprint, and put my head down and heaved the bike forward as hard as I could. But there was no jump left in my legs, and halfway up the straight my opponent broke sharply to the left and wound up his desperate lunge for the line. I was beaten right then. Suddenly, I felt how tired I was. I decided I'd settle for second and stopped sprinting. With just 50m to go, I sat up to savour the moment.

As I rode up to the line, people seemed to be shouting but I couldn't hear them. I was in a golden reverie of pride: I had ridden like a real racing cyclist. I had attacked, and attacked again. I'd made the moves. It was, more than anyone's, more even than my winning rival's, *my* race. Whether I had come first or second felt irrelevant.

Right then, one of the riders we'd left for dead a lap before came careening past. That was why people had been shouting: they'd seen me slow up so much that the remnant of our earlier break was catching up fast. One of them had caught me and taken second place. I was squeezed into third place.

— You great wally, Andy shouted at me, unable to suppress the huge grin on his face. — Didn't you hear us yelling at you? We were telling you to look out behind and get a move on. You should have got second.

I shrugged with as much insouciance as I could muster.

— Yeah, I know, but I haven't got a sprint. And I still got a point.

— You can't think like that, Andy went on. — You should have *won* it. You were the strongest rider.

— Shame. But well done . . . It looked like a good ride, said Mick quietly, sympathetic but amused.

I had to admit to myself that it was embarrassingly negligent. An elementary mistake. And in front of all those people. I'd ridden a great race, only to make an utter fool of myself in the last hundred yards. More than that, I had found a flaw in my competitive instinct. In an instant, off the bike, the brief glow of glory was all but forgotten. When I replayed the last lap in my mind, I realised that I had not only allowed myself to lead out the sprint, but had also hardly contested it. Losing second place was laughably careless, but gifting first place to another was perverse. I had enjoyed making the break, but I wondered whether in some obscure way I had not wanted the win itself. Not possessing a sprint seemed an excuse to opt out of what, finally, the race was all about. I had my single point, it was true, and no longer a blank licence. I had at last come of age as a racing cyclist, but what in the end was I doing this for, if not to win?

— Do you want to know what I did today? asked Ruth, looking up from the arts section of the Sunday paper.

— Yes . . . Sure, I replied as brightly as my weary-legged lethargy permitted.

She paused slightly, so that I knew that my curiosity about how she had spent her day had better be sincere.

— Well, I got up about nine, had a bath, and then went to a screening at 10.30 . . .

— What was the film? I asked, seizing on the opportunity to show interest.

— An action-adventure thing with Ray Liotta. It was crap. *Really* stupid. Not even good crap, just crap crap.

— Still . . . *Ray Liotta*, right?

The actor Ray Liotta, marked by bad skin, piercing blue eyes and dangerous charisma, was the nearest thing I had to a rival in our relationship. After his performances as a sexy psychotic in *Something Wild* and apprentice wiseguy in *Goodfellas*, Liotta had become Ruth's main screen idol. She even interviewed him once. Lounging in the hotel room, he turned the tables flirtatiously and started asking the questions. 'Did anyone ever tell you, you look like Faye Dunaway?' Audibly reduced to a blushing teenager, Ruth managed a mumbled deprecation and was then, for once, stuck for words. He savoured the moment, his voice laconic, drawling. 'Because . . . you know . . . you have the same hair and everything.' He chuckled ambiguously.

I knew this because Ruth had kept the tape of the encounter.

— He keeps making terrible movies. Dumb management, dumb guy. I'm through with him.

— Does he know you've dumped him? I asked, with mock concern.

— Funny. Anyway, I had a cappuccino and a chocolate croissant in the Häagen-Dazs café with Nicki. And then I went up to Louise's.

— And how is *she*?

— Oh, you know, all right. Depressed.

— Uh-huh. And then you came home?

— Yeah, finished a piece. Ate some biscuits. Read the paper.

— Anything interesting?

— One thing: a piece about Versace and masculinity, by Elizabeth Wilson. A sort of decoding. Clever – don't know why no one else writes about fashion like that. About what fashion means, clothes as cultural symbols – instead of the usual fluff.

— I should read it . . .
— So did you win?
— Nah.

Did I *finish* would have been a more informed enquiry, but this question had become ritualistic. I was never certain how ironic it was intended to be. She could not really know how difficult it was to win a race, to be first out of 60 racers. And yet she did know I never won; she must have had some inkling of how long the odds were.

— I did finish . . . third. I should have got second, but I did get my first point.

— That's good, she said.

It was a kind of willed ignorance at which we both connived: she was really not that interested in my racing, and I did not want her to be. If there was an edge of mockery in the question 'Did you win?', it cut both ways. Its deliberate obtuseness contained a hint of her sense of the absurdity of the enterprise; at the same time, an acknowledgement that it was an exclusive, male rite, and something which was therefore not given to her to understand. Racing was my domain, an autonomous region, a place to escape to.

It strikes me how happy we were, sharing our lives yet going our separate ways every Sunday. Trusting one another, but scarcely curious about how each had filled the intervening hours.

Stage 4

Tomorrow the bicycle races
Through the suburbs on summer
*   evenings. But today the struggle.*
                    — W. H. Auden

Cycling separately from work, we met at King's, at the foot of Denmark Hill. I came from Pimlico, from the small London office of *The New Yorker* magazine, and Ruth further, from Canary Wharf where she was an editor at the *Independent*. Our destination was by then familiar to us: the hospital's Assisted Conception Unit. By an unthinking administrative irony, the ACU occupied a small complex a couple of floors directly below the maternity ward. In the gurney-sized lifts that served the lumpishly utilitarian sixties block, pale, tense-faced women who wished they could have children rubbed shoulders with heavily-laden, huffing women who, you might guess, half-wished they weren't just about to.

There was no waiting room in the ACU, only a wide corridor with a line of chairs along one wall. Though no doubt dictated as before by blind bureaucratic exigency, this arrangement at least was a mercy in disguise. It meant that visitors to the ACU could only sit in profile to one another; no one beside the staff had to endure the blend of hope and sorrow written on the faces of those attending the clinic. And, like medical personnel everywhere, the staff seemed immune to this infectious mood, inoculated by sheer routine against the bacillus of anxiety and disappointment. On the wall, among the public health posters and information leaflets, was one pinboard reserved for photographs – sent in by lucky winners, the thankful parents – of babies beaming with gratitude at having begun life in a King's petri dish. Next to them a stapled sheaf of tables and graphs was pinned to the board. This, you realised once you had deciphered the statistics, gave the clinic's figures for the diminishing returns of IVF, by age group and number of attempts. First try, for our age group: a success rate of 15 per cent. That was the starting price. Thereafter, the odds would only get longer.

— He's taking his time, I hissed sotto voce to Ruth.

— Shh! she retorted, indicating with a nod the man's partner just a couple of chairs down the corridor from us.

There was a queue for the *men's room* at the ACU. We were there to see the consultant, but I was also due to provide a sperm sample for testing. Since our infertility was unexplained, I could easily have been the culprit with a low count, poor motility . . . who knew? However much you tell yourself otherwise, it is hard for any man entirely to dissociate the notion of fertility from the idea of potency. You know you should know better, but it goes to the heart of how you feel it is to be a man; you do not want to be found inadequate. I did not let on how nervous I was about what the test might show. Until proven innocent, I assumed some guilt. I just wanted to get it over with.

King's *had* a men's room. This was considered progressive, even a luxury, since it meant that someone somewhere within the health service officialdom had actually given sympathetic consideration to the question of exactly how and where men should be expected to *produce* their sperm samples. But the facility comprised just one small room, and you had to wait until it was your turn, when a nurse would issue you with the key to the room. It seemed a laborious process all round. After a further few minutes of delay, my impatience got the better of me.

— Right. I'm not hanging around any longer.

— Where are you going? Ruth asked, a little alarmed.

— I'm going to use the loo, I said and stalked off up the corridor.

If queuing for the men's room seemed depressing, then the disinfectant-scrubbed dinginess of the men's toilets was hardly an improvement. But there was no going back now with an empty sample bottle.

Miles. Doing the miles. Getting the miles in. This was the lingua franca of racing cyclists. More even than places and points when the season has started, the number of miles you'd done in training was the standard by which you were measured by your peers. Miles earned respect, because everyone understood that results counted for less than a commitment to sheer dogged effort. Category mattered up to a point, but once you'd reached first cat status, it was assumed you had attained a certain minimum of racing mettle. After that, you earned respect purely for the way you rode and for how you raced – whether you were willing to *work*.

If you had done the miles, then it was taken for granted that you had been out hard-riding in all weathers in the off-season, probably on both weekend days and at least one weekday evening. If there were some reason I could not make the Wednesday evening run, there were occasions when I would get up instead at 5.30 in the dark of a February morning, so that I could get a two-hour ride done before work. To get the miles in.

Over time my attitude modified. In my first years of winter training, before I was racing, I would join the club run religiously every Sunday morning. Some of us met at Crystal Palace, but rendezvoused again with other riders in Bromley, including a man named Tony. Tony was bigger than most riders, and looked ungainly on his bike. Even riding steady on the flat his body rocked around arythmically; when he got out of the saddle on a climb, his bike lurched from side to side, so that he looked like some huge insect struggling with its prey. Tony was about as unpretty a rider as you would ever see in the bunch, but for him this total lack of style didn't seem to diminish his power. When I first joined, he was the club's only first cat rider. He possessed a formidable sprint, plenty of racing experience, and a fiercely competitive urge. At one time he was the national motor-paced champion.

In the early days of cycle racing, there was a great motor-paced race from Bordeaux to Paris. For most of the race, the competitors would be strung out behind a large motorbike, getting towed along in its slipstream for several hundred miles at an absolutely blistering pace, only for the motorbike to peel off as the race neared its destination to leave the few survivors to battle it out over the final miles. I would almost shudder to read about it: it sounded so grimly purgatorial. Motor-pacing nowadays is exclusively a track activity: two riders race off one against another, starting on opposite sides, over a set number of laps; each rides tightly tucked in behind a low-slung motorbike on which the driver sits very upright behind long handlebars to create a hole in the wind for the rider behind. There are special bikes for motor-paced racing, with smaller front wheels and reversed forks to enable the racer to ride right up against the metal roller which buffers any accidental contact between motorbike and bicycle. The motorbikes would rumble round with a muted roar like cruising Harleys, gradually picking up the pace for the cyclist behind. At full race pace, the speeds are so extreme that the riders turn what would otherwise be an impossibly big gear; even then, sustaining more than 40mph, their legs spin at very high revs. Because it was such a specialised event, being the national champion did not equate to being, say, the national road race champion. To ride so close to a heavy motorbike, your wheel right on the roller, was not for the faint-hearted and only a few were brave enough to do it.

As well as an unusual combination of speed and stamina, Tony rode with the utter fearlessness that is bred of a supreme confidence in one's own competence, but which can appear from the outside a recklessness bordering mild psychosis. Once, on a grey winter's day's training ride, I was fifty or sixty yards behind him pedalling like crazy to keep up down a country road that was brown with mud from farm vehicles, now made slick by heavy overnight rain. We were at the fastest section of this twisting descent when a van pulled out of a side-road right in front of Tony. A poor rider would have hit the back of it; even a good rider would have locked his wheels trying to avoid it and come off. Inches from a sickening collision Tony just flicked his bike across the white lines and overtook the van. When I caught up with him at the foot of the hill, I was still shaking. He showed no sign of nerves and said nothing of it. But with Tony, at the best of times, conversation was barely sustainable if it was not bike talk.

Because of his status, Tony took charge of the club runs. Every Sunday he would take us on 70-mile excursions into Kent, up and down all the hills he could think of. As we rode in on the flat A-road back to Bromley, he liked to wind up the pace, ending in a sprint for a particular lamppost just before his turn-off home. The rest of us, central London dwellers, then had another ten miles, including the climb back over Crystal Palace, before we could rest our weary, lactic-filled legs and enjoy a warm bath. It became routine for me to clock up 90 miles on these runs, rides which left me very nearly comatose for the remainder of the day. In mid-winter it might almost be dark when I got home; and it had barely been light when I left. Tony's club runs were a crash course in cycling masochism.

Later, as Mick and I both gained experience and needed to fit our training into otherwise increasingly busy lives, we came to realise that, when it came to miles, quality mattered at least as much as quantity. A two-hour ride which comprised an hour at close to full-out effort, averaging at least 20mph, would be of greater benefit than four hours steady-state pedalling, averaging 14 or 15mph. With the advent of pulse monitors and a sports-science-derived approach to training, the old wisdom that simply being on your bike for hours monotonously cranking out the miles was *the* way came to be seen as anachronistic. Mick and I would exchange knowing remarks about the dangers of *overtraining*. It happened: there were riders we knew who ended up sick or injured because they'd flogged themselves, training in the cold and wet with not enough in the bottle and not enough on their backs. The symptoms might be anything from plain fatigue and a paradoxical lack of form, to tendonitis or a kidney infection. But there were always some who preferred the old ways. One of the toughest riders in our division broke all the rules by getting off his bike entirely for two or three months after the end of the season. By January he'd be pounds heavier than he'd been at the end of September. But then he would climb back on his bike and train every day, clocking up thousands of miles, punishing himself whatever the weather until, by the end of February, he was ready to race again. For him, it worked. There was no science involved. It was just graft. The truth was that we all remained in thrall to the atavistic draw of spending hours in the saddle. However much you read up about modern methods in the training manual, we all knew the way to improve was to get the miles in.

There was no hiding from the logic that to go faster you had to ride your bike. Even when the winter darkness and poor weather discouraged one from getting out to do miles on the road, there was always the turbo-trainer. Everyone has limits, but usually the mental ones are reached long before the physical. Training was often lonely and dull, mind-numbingly dull. For instance: however much I wanted the fitness, I could rarely compel myself to use the turbo-trainer; Mick, on the other hand, was an assiduous user. Sometimes it was only the thought of being left behind by him – and there it was again, the competitive bedrock of our cycling comradeship – that drove me to it. The turbo-trainer is a stationary device on which you park your bike, usually by taking out the front wheel and dropping the forks into a slot that could be tightened with a skewer-lever; the rear wheel would rest on rollers. You sit and pedal, going nowhere, and the machine works by providing resistance created by a fan (hence *turbo*). In effect, it turns your everyday road bike into an exercise bike.

Most stands fold up for storage, so you can keep them *in your closet*, as they say on the shopping channel. You can use the turbo-trainer anywhere you want, so long as whoever you live with can tolerate its tedious hum. But the cooler the place, the better: after a few minutes of steady pedalling, you start to sweat. Stationary, indoors, you do not have the crucial airflow that naturally cools you when you are actually in motion on a bike. First, the beads prickle at your temples, then droplets join to make rivulets which stream down your brows and collect in mini-dams made by your eyebrows. Eventually the flood bursts and the salty liquid spills into your eyes before dripping off your nose and chin. Even after a brief half-hour session, your body would still be popping perspiration an hour later in the effort to cool itself down. If you were lucky enough to have a garage, that is where you would use a turbo-trainer. But stuck in a London maisonette, I would put down an old towel in the living room to catch the sweat. Later I bought a small electric fan. The cooling draft it provided helped a little, but by the end of a workout, my skin would be stinging from the salinity of my evaporated sweat.

Turbo-training was an impoverished experience in virtual cycling. There was something of the absurd about it. Here you were, pumping out perhaps hundreds of watts for the best part of an hour, power that was simply being wasted in air resistance, noise and body heat; you would even be using electricity to run the fan that was cooling you down, and to play music via headphones to prevent your brain atrophying with boredom. As you mopped up the slick of sweat on the floor afterwards, you could not help feeling that there would be a little more point to the exercise if at least the turbo-trainer were hitched up to a small generator.

I'd bought the turbo-trainer from Andy second-hand for £25. For most of its life, this turbo-trainer stood up against the wall in a passageway, half-covered with hanging coats and jackets. I took it out only if absolutely desperate to train because turbo-training came to be hateful to me. It was pure distilled boredom. At least Sisyphus had had the satisfaction of shouldering the boulder to the top of the hill, even if it always rolled down again. With the turbo-trainer, you go nowhere, achieve nothing. All you do is burn invisible calories and raise your pulse. Unlike a normal bike with its own momentum, there was no flywheel effect, just dead resistance. As soon as you stopped pedalling, you would come to a halt. The turbo-trainer demanded constant effort, keeping you somewhere just below the threshold of pain, but at a level of discomfort that was maddeningly distracting. There was no room for your mind to wander pleasantly, the way it can when you're swimming laps in a pool or jogging round a park. Like many others, Mick used a turbo-trainer in tandem with a pulse monitor for maximum efficiency. I tried this too: at least the little blinking numbers on the wristwatch-like device gave you something to focus on besides your discomfort. The pulse monitor allowed you to create artificial goals, to do *intervals* – cycles of brief intense effort (typically at around 90 per cent of maximum heart-rate) and recovery periods. Even so, the sheer boredom was far more killing than the effort of maintaining a minute at 175 beats per minute. To get round the monotony of the turbo-trainer, I would screw up my eyes and try to visualise a favourite hill, a long steady climb. I would imagine pounding up it in an aggressive tempo. Even so, a mere five minutes seemed like an hour. The turbo-trainer was an infernal version of H. G. Wells's time-machine which, instead of clocking through centuries, had the effect of slowing time almost to a standstill.

Pulse monitoring, though, was the way forward. There was no doubting its efficiency; over a short period, it could give an edge to your form that unscientific training almost certainly could not. Not only would monitoring your pulse tell you whether you were doing enough work to improve your fitness, but it could also tell you when your body needed to recover – when you shouldn't be working at all, but resting. The American Greg Lemond was probably the first cycling champion produced by pure sports science, but his Spanish successor, the dominant pro of the early nineties, Miguel Indurain seemed to belong even more to the future. Indurain – his very name sounded like a brand name for something preternaturally tough and lasting – rode almost without a flicker of expression on his face. He rode almost without tactics; just a single strategy, which was to destroy the rest of the field in the time trials. Seeming to exist in some scarcely human realm of pure performance, there was something cyborg-like about him. We read over and over that Indurain's lung capacity was twice that of an average mortal, that his heart was half as large again, and that his pulse at rest maintained a metronomic 28bpm – less than half that of a fit normal person. Indurain was the incarnation of the athlete's dream of himself as more machine than man.

Before Lemond and Indurain, no one had cared what, say, Stephen Roche's pulse-rate was. From pros down to club cyclists, riders simply talked of having *good legs* one day, and *bad legs* another. Now, because of Indurain's magic number, racing cyclists became obsessed with measuring their resting pulse-rates. They would lie still in their beds every morning just after waking, with their fingers pressed to their wrists and their eyes on the second-hand of their watch, trying to breathe as evenly as in sleep and without moving a limb. Where once clubmates had talked about how many miles they had done that week, now they swapped resting pulse-rates. It was a type of validation for the choices we had made. Life would feel worthwhile if your resting pulse had dropped from 46 to 42.

For a memorable period in the early nineties, the battle between the old ways and the new was dramatised by the competition between two British time-triallists, Graeme Obree and Chris Boardman. Obree had built his strange-looking bike while on the dole, cannibalising parts not just from other bikes but even, famously, from an old washing machine. His training was all solitary road miles. His bike and the position he took on it looked eccentric, but Obree was an old-fashioned British cyclist to the core. For his part, Boardman was never without his coach, a sports scientist. He too used an unorthodox bike, but a hi-tech, wind-tunnel-tested machine specially manufactured from carbon fibre. Like any cyclist, Boardman did miles, but he also trained on rollers hooked up to a computer that measured his power output, pulse-rate, oxygen consumption, lactate production – whatever could be scientifically measured. As these two cyclists duelled for cycling's blue riband, the *hour* record (simply, the greatest distance a cyclist can travel around a track in one hour), what was at stake symbolically were whole philosophies: tradition versus modernity, amateur versus professional, intuition versus science. Technically, Boardman won the bout when Obree's mark was rubbed out by the ruling of the Union Cycliste Internationale (cycle sport's governing body) that Obree's riding position and bike were illegal. At the time, however, Obree was the more popular among club cyclists, and to many the moral victor. His bike may have been newfangled, but in spirit he represented the sort of cycling they knew and the old wisdom that the only way to improvement was through hard work and long miles.

Obree flirted briefly with a professional career, but his very individualism seemed to thwart him in that course. Boardman, by contrast, launched his immaculately by winning gold on the track at the Barcelona Olympics. Boardman came from the Wirral in the north-west, so I had never seen him race, but if you read *the comic* – as the weekly bulletin *Cycling News* was known by racing cyclists everywhere, with mingled affection and contempt – you knew who he was. Week after week, he topped the time-trial results with improbably low times in *10s* and *25s*. After Barcelona, I wanted to admire him as a champion for British cycling – at last we had a modern figurehead. So when he fell on slippery cobbles in his first Tour prologue time trial and broke his ankle, I felt the bitterness of his disappointment almost as my own. I knew something of what it felt like to crash out of a race when your hopes were high – at least I could imagine how significant a moment that should have been in his career. But thereafter, whenever interviewed by the media, Boardman always seemed preoccupied with his pulse-rate. It seemed virtually his only topic for comment; too often it sounded like an excuse. Now, after his retirement from professional racing, I can see he deserved more respect and sympathy. It seems plain that he was one of the few *clean* cyclists in the peloton. Little wonder that he was always hunting for some physiological explanation for his apparent lack of form, for why he seemed so often to be struggling to keep pace with lesser talents. They were using EPO and growth hormones; he was riding on vitamins.

As always, to keep up with Mick, I flirted with pulse monitoring. I bought one from a friend and used it for a time, but with little more enthusiasm than I used the turbo-trainer – and usually only in tandem with it. Besides the chunky wristwatch-style display, you had to wear a thick elasticated strip around your chest holding in place a plastic-housed sensor to pick up the electrical impulses of the heartbeat. I never wore it enough to become accustomed to it, so it felt constrictive and uncomfortable, like having to wear a too-stiff collar and tie. When the battery went flat, I didn't replace it.

With a silent sigh of relief, I stashed the pulse monitor away and forgot about it. You shouldn't need a pulse monitor, I decided – you should be able to push yourself without resort to artificial means, clinical methods. You know when you have good legs and when you don't. You should be able to ride by feel and instinct and experience. As if on cue, or in a final, embittered acknowledgement of my loathing, the turbo-trainer immolated itself. With a sudden apocalyptic clatter, the blades on its plastic fan disintegrated, rendering useless the rest of its rusting frame. It went, unmourned, to the municipal dump.

After that, I preferred to train on the road, even if it meant contending with bad weather and winter darkness. On the road there was something to occupy the mind, to save one from the fate of the gerbil running on a treadmill. Even the escape from the city through the endless suburban streets seemed, for all its familiarity, infinitely more appealing. There was always the lure and reward of the countryside; even the shortest training ride – two hours, out and back – would give up a taste of the scenery, landscape, fresh sights and smells that belonged to the North Downs and that, for an hour, would belong to me. Just that brief private freedom felt sufficient to sustain me through a week's ordinary life in the city. As long as I had the time, I preferred doing the miles.

It was Saturday afternoon and we were visiting Ruth's sister's for tea. Justine is good at tea; it is a rite she believes in almost religiously. Tea was fine with me. I would be racing the next day, but I could allow myself some cake and biscuits, provided I didn't lose my appetite for a big pasta supper later. Carbo-loading, and resting my legs, were the imperatives to which my thoughts kept returning, a constant refrain at the back of my mind.

Ruth often brought flowers. Sometimes we would bring pastries as well, but there were always teacakes or muffins or a cake there in any case. Justine's son was a boisterous four-year-old. Big for his age, a real boy, charging in and out, raiding the slices of buttered malt loaf on the kitchen table.

Justine was pregnant, expecting her second child. It shouldn't have mattered, but the mere fact subtly underscored our apparent incapacity. In the space of what seemed just a few weeks, this circumstance had escalated from little more than an excuse for an indefinite future free from contraception to a full-scale existential crisis. Ruth and I were gradually being forced to contemplate what our lives together might look like without the kind of planned domestic chaos that having children seemed to make so desirable. A life for which a weekly visit to her sister's provided a vivid snapshot.

I had always assumed – though only in a loose, abstract way – that this would mark a natural caesura in our lives. I understood, in this same abstract way, that having children would mean retiring from racing. I supposed that I would feel ready for that decision when the moment came; it had always seemed far enough off. Now, however, I was confronted by the confusing possibility that I might never have to give up; I could go on cycling for ever. Was that what I really wanted? It was hard to banish the superstitious thought that perhaps I should have been more careful what I had wished for; that perhaps some divine agency had seen into my heart, found my secret disloyalty and, in the cold ironic spirit of providential justice, granted my hidden desire.

Like an ultra-sound scan, the uncertainty about whether we would be able to have children had revealed occluded fault-lines in our relationship. Our attitudes had started suddenly to diverge. I was still sanguine. Ruth was bound to get pregnant sooner or later. I didn't mind doing the tests and taking whatever measures resulted, but I did not feel the urgency. We had still to hit thirty, both of us. Young enough yet.

For Ruth, it was different. She knew she had time, in a technical sense. But it was the possible emptiness of all that time ahead that was forcing a reckoning for her; she felt the need to face up to a childless future *right now*. Where I was happy to postpone the disappointment, she wanted to tackle the emotion head-on: mourn the children she could never have, if that was what was to be.

It worried me how out of sync we had become. I was bewildered by the way she had moved in a short space of time from relative indifference to having children, even ambivalence about it, to a place where it had become a blight on our lives, a deep source of welling anguish and sorrow. Trying to adjust to the force of Ruth's feelings was like being in a small boat caught in a squall. I cursed my folly for not seeing the bad weather coming. At the same time I had to swallow my impatience at all this expenditure of feeling on so shaky a premise. It seemed illogical to be unhappy so prematurely, before we even knew for certain whether we had cause to be.

— The doctor . . . I didn't like her: she was a cold, judgmental bitch . . . Ruth told her sister. — She said I may have to have more tests.

— What sort of tests? asked Justine.

— They do this thing called a laparoscopy where they open you up, stick a periscope in and have a look at your insides. It means a general anaesthetic, but not an overnight stay.

— So when will this have to happen?

— After we get the other results back: my hormone tests and Matt's sperm test. Provided those are normal. She shot a sideways look at me. — Obviously, I don't get to have a laparoscopy if they show Matt's firing blanks.

— *Excuse* me, I said.

— Well, it could be you, you know, Ruth said briskly. — We just don't know yet.

— Perhaps all that cycling ... it can't be good for *your* fertility, offered Justine.

— Hold on ...

— That's right, joined Ruth. — Too much heat kills sperm, doesn't it? Like tight jeans are supposed to cause low sperm counts.

— And what could be tighter than cycle shorts? Justine added.

— And all those hours on those tiny saddles, said Ruth. — There was an article in one of your cycling magazines about how cycling can cause *penile numbness* and *erectile dysfunction*. A faint archness in her voice inflected the technical terms.

— Oh great, so now I'm impotent as well as infertile! Aren't we jumping to conclusions here?

— Well, think about it, said Ruth. — It is possible, isn't it? Why does it have to be something wrong with me? And we did get pregnant once, remember, before you were so into cycling.

— That was years ago. We were practically still teenagers. Everybody's fertile then. The hormones are coming out of your ears.

— But what if it *was* you? Would you give up cycling? Ruth insisted.

— Well ... yeah. I guess. I mean, I'd have to, wouldn't I? ... But I don't accept that there's a link between cycling and low sperm counts. What about professional cyclists? They spend far more time in the saddle than I do, but I've never heard anything about pros not being able to have children.

My audience remained sceptical.

— OK, so if it's me, if I have a low sperm count, I'll give up cycling. OK? Now can we change the subject please?

The conversation turned to something in the papers. Though

indignant about the way my cycling had been impugned, I felt a little uneasy about the promise I'd made. The seed of doubt had been planted. What if it *was* me?

I had to ask myself: would I really be prepared to give up cycling? I could give up almost anything without much sense of privation. But cycling?

Fitness cannot be faked. You might hear one of the old boys talking wishfully sometimes about *muscle memory* – the idea that your legs will remember what to do even after a long lay-off. They may remember the feel, but fitness they forget. No amount of natural ability can substitute for a lack of form. This was one of the things I loved about cycling: it repaid work; it rewarded dogged effort. With fitness comes stamina: through long-term training, you alter your physiology. The body's metabolism adapts its chemistry to the stresses to which it is forced to become accustomed.

Your heart grows stronger and more efficient. Your lungs increase in size and their capacity to exchange oxygen. The muscles in your legs learn to tolerate ever-higher levels of lactic acid – the toxic waste produced by your muscles' combustion of its glycogen fuel. When gym evangelists rhapsodise about *feeling the burn*, they're referring to the pain of lactic acid building up in tired muscles. But there is nothing you can do in a gym that would even approximate to the way your legs hurt after 80 miles at race pace, when you have to ride hard up a sharp hill for the fourth or fifth time, and then sprint over the top just at the moment you would want to sit back and soft-pedal to recover.

This always happens in races: the splits come not at the bottom of the climb, nor even halfway up, but over the top, just when you think you are safe, that you've made the necessary effort. That is when you have to be vigilant, prepared to go again. A 10-foot deficit at the peak of the climb, the place where on the Continent someone will have painted a *prime* line across the road for the *grimpeurs*, translates into an unbridgeable 100-foot crevass on the flat within seconds. A moment's weakness or loss of concentration and you could be chasing to rejoin the bunch for the next mile or two. Nothing, you would think, could be worse than the pain of having to sprint to stay on – until you have experienced the pain of chasing for all you're worth, with the humiliation of being *off the back* snapping at your heels.

And all the time, the pain is telling you to stop. That is what pain is for: the warning sign, a red alert. But to race, you have to find the will to hurt yourself more, to *feel the burn*. The pain is exquisite, enveloping, consuming. You are aware of little else. Your vision narrows to a tunnel where nothing intrudes save the need to follow the wheel in front of you and close the gap. There is just the pain and your will to overcome it.

Cycle-racing does differ in this from marathon-running, for instance, where the effort is generally steady and constant. There might be tactical changes of pace for marathon runners, but they must also steel themselves to endure an endless-seeming grind of discomfort. In a bike race, there is an unpredictable cycle of brief periods of extreme intensity and moments of respite: *longeurs* when nothing much is happening at all and you might even exchange a fleeting comment with another rider; periods of recovery when you hide in the bunch, praying that your legs will feel better by the time the hammer goes down again; intense, short spurts followed by effortless freewheeling when some rider who is being closely marked feints an attack and then backs off; then long spells at a steady, high pace, when there is a chase being organised at the front which you merely follow. Sometimes it is almost a relief to go on the attack and get in a break, for then the effort settles to a level just below the threshold of real hurt where you have more control in managing your effort. You work as hard as you can without slipping into oxygen debt.

There were moments in races when I could have laid my head down on my handlebars and nodded off, where the grass verge looked so verdant and lush that it looked like an emerald-green mattress left out for me to lie down and sleep upon. Sometimes I was short of sleep, but when you are at that peak of fitness, you find that you need less. In summer, I'd be up early to race, earlier still in winter to train, forcing down a large bowl of porridge while it was still dark outside. Half-woken by my alarm, Ruth would issue the testy *shush* she normally reserved for persistent chatterers in the cinema and then turn back to the wall for her full quota of slumber.

My sleepiness in the saddle may have been an effect of the endorphins, the body's natural tranquillisers, released by hard exercise. A race would normally start with a flurry of activity, with everyone jockeying for position, and perhaps an early attack. Straight away you would be *on the rivet* – an expression dating from the old days when all bike saddles had Brooks-style rivets securing the leather at the back. To be on the rivet meant you were stretched out over your bike, hands on the drops, torso as low as possible, with your arse worked to the back of the saddle bracing yourself to get every available ounce of leverage with each pedal stroke.

Responding to the stimulus of intense effort, your brain would flood your body with endorphins. These exercise-narcotics are the pay-off for the physical discomfort of pushing yourself to the red line. When the race hit a lull, the feel-good opiates brought a buzz of well-being that was almost post-coital in the embrace of its somnolent warm glow. But the lulls in races rarely lasted more than a few minutes, sometimes only seconds. Then more pain.

— Fahk me! Look at that. It's fahkin pathetic.

Shaun was sitting, slumped and round-shouldered, on a bench in the changing room at the end of a two-day stage race. Wearing only a sweat-soaked vest, he was naked from the waist down.

It had been a hard race. It was an observable fact that the races got harder as the season went on. In the early season, not all the bunch was up to speed; by mid-summer everyone was as fit as they were going to be that year. This had been one of those September days still hot when the sun came out, but cool, a northerly breeze presaging autumn when the sun disappeared behind a cloud. The salt of my dried sweat was encrusted behind my ears and had left white tidemarks on my jersey.

I glanced over to see what Shaun was talking about.

— I've gotta give up this racing. Look what it does to ya! I've been robbed of my fahkin manhood.

It was true, what he said. It happened to all of us. Partly it was the chilling effect of evaporating perspiration and constant cooling airflow that shrank your genitals. But it was also because all the blood was diverted from non-essential needs to the one function that mattered: driving the engine of your leg muscles. And several hours of sitting on a racing saddle probably did not help.

— Where's your *soigneuse*, then, Shaun? Someone quipped.

— Yeah, right. Chance would be a fine thing.

No one had a *soigneuse*, in fact. It would have been regarded as pretentious beyond belief. You felt sorry enough for the few girlfriends who just came to watch. Around the village halls that often doubled as changing rooms, they became the object of other cyclists' furtive looks in a half-curious, half-predatory way – the defensive postures of a male society that expected its apartheid to be inviolate.

— Too late for that anyway, added Shaun. — This one needs a fahkin crash team, not a massage.

This was his last word on the matter as he heaved himself towards the showers.

In real life, Shaun was a postie. He had also been a triathlete. This seemed to explain his tireless will to train. Triathlon tends to attract obsessive-compulsive types for whom supreme fitness in one discipline is not enough. They are stamina fetishists with an abnormal ability to withstand not only the annihilating pain of extreme endurance training, but its crushing boredom as well.

You would meet these guys from time to time. Elite triathletes often used road-racing as part of their training programmes. Their strength and fitness were phenomenal, even by the demanding standards of first-cat club racers, but they tended to be tactically naïve. You would often find them at the head of affairs towing the bunch steadily up to a break, only for a flurry of fresh-legged riders to peel off as soon as contact had been made. The triathletes hardly seemed to care: they were not there for places, or even to show off, just for the workout. We bikies would shake our heads in disbelief at these pointless displays of power-riding.

Shaun was different. He had defected fully from triathlon and gone native. The first time I saw him race was in an end-of-season meeting at the Crystal Palace circuit. No one knew him, so no one took it seriously when he rode away from the bunch right from the gun. It looked an impossible, doomed adventure.

Within a couple of laps Shaun had caught the juniors, who

always started with a half-lap advantage. Without pausing, he just rode straight past them; one of them managed to cling to his wheel for a few circuits, before falling away. The pace of the bunch behind was high because, being the last race of the year, there were primes for cash every lap. But no one wanted to commit to an all-out chase because everyone assumed the unknown rider would be reeled in automatically after another couple of laps. It was inconceivable that anyone out on their own would not blow up after a few laps.

Shaun stayed away for the entire race, a performance so awesome that one could hardly begrudge the fact that he hauled in all but three of the prime prizes. It was we who had been tactically naïve; he had known exactly what he was about.

After that, he was a marked man, a rider you'd always look out for. His instinct was always to be on the attack, so he would often be in the early moves. Because of this he didn't always enjoy the best of company, the better riders biding their time, but if Shaun was in a break you knew that it had some potential simply because he'd be driving it. He would work like a navvy himself, setting a relentless pace and meting out a tongue-lashing to anyone not pulling his weight. He could make professional sledging sound like polite dinner-party conversation. But you had to think twice before committing yourself to a break with Shaun in it: he often rode like a *super-domestique*, not to win for himself, but to soften up the opposition so that a teammate could make the decisive move later.

Being a postie meant that Shaun would have been up early and done his day's work before most people would be breaking for lunch. Then he would be out on his bike. Five or six hours in the saddle, six or seven days a week. Summer and winter. Most of us would be glad if we hadn't put on too many pounds over Christmas. By the beginning of February, a full month before the season starts in earnest, Shaun would have done 2,000 miles since the New Year.

Many of these miles would be solo. If you were feeling strong, you might go for a training ride with Shaun, but you went knowing that you risked being worked over. He trained as much as any self-respecting pro. Maybe more, because a pro would probably have a coach making sure he didn't overtrain. Shaun was made of other stuff.

Much later, after I had retired from racing, I saw Shaun one day at the track. I was passing by Herne Hill, on some errand one early summer Saturday morning. I had the children with me in the car. They were not yet three, but I thought I might stop by, show them the cyclists, see if there was anyone around I still knew, show them the children.

Shaun was sitting in the stands with a couple of mates, his feet up on row of seats in front.

— Hi, Shaun, I said.

— Hey Matt . . . How're ya doin? Where've you been?

— Fine . . . you know. Not riding much these days . . . These two keep me a bit busy, I said, nodding towards the little boy on my hip, and my daughter who was gripping on to the leg of my jeans.

Shaun did a double-take, like he hadn't noticed before.

— Those are your kids? Fahk me . . . and I thought you was a poof.

— *Me?* Not me, I said, laughing but embarrassed, a little offended. Always a revelation to discover how others see us. It was not prejudice on Shaun's part, just frank surprise that he'd misread me. He had never said anything pejorative or unkind to me when we raced together. When you are a bikie, you tend to be judged by how you ride, and that alone. As long as you are in the saddle, the rest of your life falls away.

— You not riding today? I asked, to change the subject.

— Nah. Got knee trouble. Got to rest it, replied Shaun.

— Uh, sorry. That's a drag. How long's it going to take to mend?

— Three or four weeks. I can ride on it now, but just real easy; no serious training.

I did a quick mental calculation: he wouldn't be racing again till early June. He'd be lucky to be fit again in time for the divisional champs. I felt sorry for him. He was toughing it out, acting casual, but if it were me, underneath I'd be angry and depressed about being laid up, losing my hard-earned fitness. All those miles over the winter gone to waste; it would have driven me to despair. This moment of empathy, or projection of myself into his life, brought in its wake an undertow of nausea. A sensation familiar from the times I had crashed or punctured out of races, I recognised the same sour taste of disappointment and frustration.

Directly then a wave of relief broke over me that, whatever else had happened, this was no longer my life. My happiness, or otherwise, was not any more measured in miles.

— Well, look, we'd better be going. Take care of yourself, I said, hitching my son up again and gathering my daughter's hand.

— Yeah, you too, mate.

Every race we did, Mick and I would say to each other, *That was hard*. Sometimes even, *That was the hardest race yet*, meaning that season. Or, if we needed a superlative, *That was the hardest race ever*. We said this, without fail, as we set off on the drive back towards London. Often it would be virtually the only thing we'd say to each other. Talking we had done on the way down, while full of nervous energy, trying to take one's mind off one's liquidised stomach. On the way home, we just wanted to rest and recuperate. Conversation used too many calories.

You couldn't keep any kind of form just by racing on Sundays. My pattern was to race at Crystal Palace on Tuesday nights and add a training ride after work on Thursdays, joining a group who met regularly in Anerley, down the hill from Palace. In the winter, before the clocks changed, the ride would take place in darkness. Then we would rely on safety in numbers, a group more visible in the dark than a single cyclist. We would ride out to Knockholt, on the ridge of the North Downs, which meant a steady climb to finish. Only the final few miles were outside the suburban sprawl of the city, and on a cold night the air temperature would plummet once you left behind the heated buildings and lit streets and entered the dark farmland. It was like swimming in the sea when you move unexpectedly from sun-warmed water to a sudden chill patch that the tides or currents have dragged from the deep.

In the summer, the ride would be extended, so that it dropped down the far side of the Downs into the valley where the M25 makes its orbit. By then, the season was well under way and these rides would take on a competitive edge, evolving into an unofficial race. We would chase along the narrow lanes that make up the Pilgrims' Way, saving something for the long hard drag back up to Badger's Mount.

Crystal Palace is the great landmark for south London cyclists. The twin transmitters, shaped with quaint modernity like scaled-down Eiffel Towers, are visible for miles along the North Downs, a beacon drawing one back towards the capital. The long climb to the top of the hill where the great iron and glass pavilion once stood was always the last obstacle for the weary-legged cyclist nearing the end of a ride. From there, you knew, it was downhill all the way home.

Crystal Palace was a landmark for cyclists for another reason. All through the racing season, as long as extended daylight allowed from May to September, there would be a weekly meet in the park. This was referred to by the contraction *Palace* — as in, *Are you doing Palace tonight?* The course made use of part of the old motor-racing circuit; though less than a mile long, it made imaginative use of the contours of the hill. Raced anti-clockwise, it consisted of a flat straight ending in a brutal left-handed hairpin, followed by a sharp right-hander giving on to a fast downhill section which ended with a sweeping left-hand bend with an adverse camber, and finally a steep climb back to the finishing straight.

It was a fast, technical circuit, which foxed you for the first few times out. You had to learn how to keep as much momentum as possible into the hairpin, lean the bike over as far as you dared and keep a tight line among all the other riders. Ideally, you wanted to be on the inside, your shoulder and helmet brushing the fronds of a weeping willow that, with an almost comic sense of the picturesque, marked the centre of the turn's radius. But the trick was to carry as much speed through the corner as possible: if you let too much speed scrub off, it was tempting to start pedalling too soon and risk grounding a pedal. Instead, you tried to keep your speed and then sprint, out of the saddle, as soon as you'd straightened up. Almost immediately you'd be at the next corner, the right-hander, and then swooping down the hill. When you reached the bottom, you had to learn to brake as little as possible before turning in to an intimidating left-hand curve where the road fell away down a steep grassy bank on the right. To get round it at maximum speed, you had to hit the apex, shaving a picket fence with your left shoulder. The camber was against you and the surface down there beneath overhanging trees would sometimes be so dusty, that if you got off the line at all you might feel your tyres twitch as the bike went fractionally sideways before gripping again. It took a modicum of courage every lap, even in the dry. In the wet, like many others, I wouldn't race at all. A damp surface always drew a gang of spectators down from the finishing straight to watch the inevitable fallers overcooking the corner or finding a slippery patch under the trees.

But the circuit's greatest challenge was the climb through the trees and back to the straight. It was not especially long, nor horribly steep; just relentless. The circuit was so short, you would hit that gradient every two minutes, your legs still burning, lungs tortured, from the last time round. The climb was always taken at full tilt, with everyone on the big ring. Invariably someone would attack or put in a hard turn at the front. Sometimes, if you were feeling good, you might take that turn yourself because it could often be better to be at the head of affairs dictating the pace, hurting yourself as much as you dared, but hurting everyone else too. But you had to judge it finely, keeping a little in reserve, or you could find yourself stuffed just at the top when someone would take advantage of your work by timing their jump just there. Generally, you tried to stay near the front but you followed wheels. Diligently, desperately, as though nothing else in the world mattered more.

It was a merciless circuit: if you weren't fully fit, it found you out very quickly. Even without an attack, the race pace was so implacably high that a selection would take place every lap. Someone would blow up, let go the wheel of the rider in front with a last gasp or grunt of defeat. To be at the back of the group was not where you wanted to be, for if someone let go in front of you, you would have to sprint to re-establish contact with the last wheel in the group. Early in the race, when there was still a large group, not yet shaken out, one rider like this might take out two or three more following his wheel.

The game you had to learn in all racing was that your resources were finite; you had to save your effort for when it was vital and for then alone. At Palace, that meant keeping a good position in the bunch by other than brute strength. The technique I honed was to use the run down the straight. By getting up on the inside and leaving braking as late as possible, you could glide past three or four riders and take the inside line round the hairpin. Sometimes it meant carving someone up a little, but there was nothing illegal about that. Sometimes you had to use your elbows a little.

Regulars at Palace knew the game. The only time I got abuse for doing this was when I rode the National Criterium Championship on the circuit. *Crits*, as they are known for short, are held on precisely this type of short, tight circuit. Because the racing is always aggressive and quick, and the fact that the riders lap every couple of minutes, crits, often held in city centres, offer some of the best spectating the sport has to offer. The riders flash by, a blur of brilliantly coloured jerseys, but you can glimpse their expressions, the focus and the pain on faces streaked with sweat and dust. The races, too, are full of incident and accident. By tradition, the Tour de France was followed by a series of criterium races, run rather like exhibition matches. Fully aware that the crits' chief purpose was to provide a parade of triumphant heroes for their adoring public, the senior riders usually fixed the results and determined how the prize money was to be divvied between teams before anyone had even mounted their bike.

In the late 1980s, crits were the one form of cycle-sport that promoters succeeded in packaging and persuading TV executives to broadcast. On the strength of its successful

Tour de France coverage, Channel 4 showed a city-centre criterium series, raced over closed roads in the heart of such cities as Glasgow, Cardiff and Sheffield. Overnight, the number of professional riders mushroomed from a couple of dozen to three or four score, as sponsors jumped in to get their business logo on a cycling jersey.

It didn't catch on as its promoters had hoped. The races were televised as a minority sport, broadcast at midnight, as though professional cycle racing in Britain were as weird and exotic as sumo wrestling. Even after two or three seasons, the TV criterium series remained vulnerable to economic change. When recession came in the early nineties, the sponsors melted away.

When I rode the nationals, in 1992, normal service had been resumed on the British pro scene. There were still a handful of sponsored pros, on fairly meagre wages, but no TV cameras. Mountain bike money was filtering in to support a few all-purpose pros who were paid to wear a team jersey for both on- and off-road racing. But many had returned to a kind of semi-pro subsistence, with a minimal day job that left as much time off as possible for training and racing. A deal with a team at least provided free kit and covered race fees and travelling expenses. The personnel remained the same – the guys who had threatened briefly to be household names: Dave Rayner, Jon Tanner, Chris Lillywhite and the like. In a few households, at any rate.

As the day of the crit champs drew nearer, my anxiety grew. In a moment of bravado, I had let myself be talked into entering. I had only, just a few weeks earlier, become a first cat – the sole amateur grade that permitted a racing encounter with pros. In the process, I had necessarily acquired a healthy respect for my immediate superiors, the first-cat strongmen in the South-East London division. In the nationals, I knew, I would be rubbing shoulders with the superiors of my superiors. Mick was not one to duck a challenge, but even he judged discretion the better part of valour in this case and opted to watch, not ride. Which did not exactly encourage me.

I always suffered nerves before riding Palace. You knew it was going to hurt. You knew your legs would burn and cramp. You knew your throat would feel singed because of the dust kicked up by the bunch. You knew that at the end you would be coughing up sputum you'd sucked into your lungs because you had been breathing too hard and fast even to spit. And you knew that the racing was always a dogfight and that the circuit would give you a few white-knuckle moments. This occasion had added tension. In any normal weekly race, I could pretty much guarantee that I'd make the selection and survive to the end. If I was feeling good, I might even chip off the front for a lap or two near the end. But in the nationals, there was a distinct possibility that I would be *shelled out* within just a couple of laps. This would be my comeuppance for the hubris of imagining I could even live with this company, let alone compete with it.

I had decided to wear not my club jersey, but a red-and-black skinsuit I'd bought off a clubmate. It seemed a shame not to be advertising the club and my amateur status, but on the bike it made sense – there was no extra weight, no flapping corners, no pointless pockets and no unnecessary layers on this warm August evening. Mick obliged by pinning on my numbers, saving me some awkward contortions.

Riders were already gathering on the line and there was only time for one quick lap before the line-up. Mick wished me luck, but I was already so deep in adrenaline swoon I hardly heard him. My heart was racing. I felt I couldn't get enough air in my lungs – and we hadn't even started. I forced myself to take some deep breaths.

The bunch was much bigger than anything I had encountered before at the circuit, full of sponsored teams and matching bikes instead of the usual ragtag mix of club jerseys and idiosyncratic machines. They all seemed to know one another and stood over their bikes chatting, as though the race were over, not just about to begin. Wondering at their nonchalance, I licked my dry mouth. As always, I wished that I had had another drink and another pee before the start. Then there was a call for silence and a brief talk from the commissaire. He gave an explanation of how the hooter would sound the start of a prime lap (utterly irrelevant to me) and a firm statement that lapped riders would be pulled out (entirely relevant to me). Then he stood back from the track, raised his right arm and fired the starter's pistol. The whiplash crack was greeted with a staccato chorus of clicks as all the riders pressed the cleat of their one loose shoe into the pedal's retaining plate. We were away.

I concentrated on staying as far up the bunch as possible, but by the time I reached the first corner, forced almost to a standstill by the funnel effect, there was already a stream of riders sprinting out of the exit. Heart thumping more from nerves than exertion I followed them out, and down the hill for the first time. Many riders new to the circuit did not know the line to take, so people were braking much more than necessary. Already blocked, I was frustrated, knowing that the more momentum lost going down, the harder we would have to sprint on the way up.

The pace was quick, but the expected blast straight from the gun that I had expected did not materialise. True, I was not even near enough the front to know what was happening up there, but the pace seemed more controlled and steady than I had expected: it was fast, but not ridiculous. By the time I reached the finishing line again, I was feeling almost comfortable. The old technique at the hairpin served me well. All the riders queued up on the outside of the bend to make the tightest line possible round the apex, but with so many of them piling up in ranks, they still had to slow right down. All I had to do was charge up the inside, while everyone was coasting towards the bend, get on the brakes as late as possible and swallow up five or six places at a swoop. There was no one to stop you taking the inside line, and the riders on the outside simply had to make way.

Some didn't like it, and grumbled: '*Oi! Watch it!*' But it was mild stuff. I didn't even look round to see where it was coming from. The manoeuvre was perfectly legal; if they didn't like it, then they could do the same as I and make their own space. After a while, I realised it was working out so well, that I could afford to let some places slip on the way up the hill and recoup at the corner. So the race went on, lap by lap. My highest goal being to survive and finish, I probably never placed higher than fifteenth during the entire race. I knew well enough that one moment of over-ambition, the folly of trying an attack or even showing at the front, would mean instant oxygen debt with no chance of recovery. I was near enough my limit as it was, without risking a finish for a moment of pyrrhic glory.

When the race's decisive move came, I had no idea. At some point in the last ten laps a breakaway formed, with enough teams represented to forestall any concerted reaction from the bunch. Occasionally, I would look over and glimpse a group of four or five rounding another part of the circuit ahead of us. Every time I looked, they were further ahead, until eventually I saw them no more. Then with three laps to go, there was suddenly a commotion behind: the breakaway group had made contact with the main field and was working their way through. The shouts were coming from the escapees who did not want to be blocked in their progress. In effect, the entire bunch was now being lapped; our race rendered irrelevant. But for the breakaways, it was a critical moment: the strongest could work their way through to the front quickly and hope that their rivals would be held up by the mass of other riders. These were moments of confusion. Were we still in the race? Should we pull over? Where *were* these riders coming through?

Theoretically we were all lapped riders then and should have been pulled out. In practice, this close to the finish, with this many riders, it would have been impossible. It was simply up to us not to impede those who were now racing through our ranks at an improbable speed. Two laps later, the routed bunch made a desultory, half-hearted gallop for the finish – a lap down on the winner: the compact, powerful figure of Chris Lillywhite.

Already my achievement – of hanging in the bunch – did not seem so spectacular. It had made me work hard, and concentrate, but it had not really hurt me. As a cyclist, you know very well the limit of your powers; it was simple logic that if I had survived the race, then Mick, and any one of the dozen other first cats who made up the weekly elite at Palace, could have done at least as well. But to see Lillywhite take his place on the makeshift podium was to be reminded of another order: how anyone could have ridden fast enough to gain a lap on that bunch was another thing entirely. You could only shake your head and wonder at what stuff these men were made of.

I rolled in towards the rear, my face streaked with sweat and dust. Inside I was aglow: I had done it. Mick ran up to me, the delight on his face mirroring my own elation. He was clapping my back as I was still rolling.

— Well done! You *finished*! That was fantastic.

A part of him must have been wishing he were in my shoes. But if he felt this, he hid it well. His sheer excitement placed the seal on my sense of pride. Only later did I suspect the part plain good luck had played in the event – the particular scenario the race had taken that permitted my survival. If a breakaway had not been allowed to go by those controlling the race, the pace would have been more uneven and far more brutal; I would soon have been jettisoned. The tactical game (in which I was just a bystander), and my local knowledge, had kept me in the race. On another circuit, or another day, it would have been a different story.

Even as things stood, my name would not have entered the most minutely conscientious journalist's account of that year's race. The photographers were probably packing their lenses by the time I crossed the line. In all likelihood, no one will even have kept the start sheet to record that I was there. Still, while other races fade and blur in the memory to a dwindling, undifferentiated mass, I cherish the evening when I rode the National Crit Champs, and finished. I was there, and it felt like the greatest day of my life.

Stage 5

Marriage is a wonderful invention; but, then again, so is a bicycle repair kit.

— Billy Connolly

— So where do you want to go for our honeymoon? Ruth asked, hitting the mute button and fixing the profile of my face with her regard.

Once we had made the decision to get married, much about it had acquired this air of humdrum administrative matters. And there were so many insignificant-seeming, but nonetheless necessary decisions to be made. All the distracting detail was like brush and undergrowth which made it more difficult to see the path we had determined on. I ought to have a sense, I felt, of participating in an event of seismic consequence. Instead, it was as though I were trapped in one of those children's playpens knee-deep in multicoloured plastic balls – buoyed up, but somehow awash and adrift.

We had always seen ourselves as an informal couple, with the notion that our bond was something renewed voluntarily each day. The vestiges of this attitude left us with a vague sense of embarrassment about inviting our family and friends to anything as formal as a wedding. We both had a need to remain slightly aloof from and ironic about the whole proceedings, to apologise for the event by placing it in inverted commas — even if an earnest motive was somewhere concealed within.

Marriage was, I rationalised, a ritual public way of re-affirming our desire to be together despite the fact that, as seemed most likely, we might not have children. The clinic had not found anything wrong with either of us, so we were none the wiser. But with every passing month we migrated further from the vague, still hopeful label of *subfertility* towards the unequivocal designation *infertility*.

The NHS waiting list for IVF was counted, then, not in years but decades. Going to a private clinic we had hardly discussed. Given IVF's fairly low rate of success, it seemed likely to cost more than we could afford to spend. In any case, at some visceral level we both still harboured moral qualms about 'going private'. We had decided to take our chances with biology for the time being. Getting married was our consolation. Or at least an acceptable rationalisation.

The real feeling we found on the wedding day surprised us. Our inclination to keep everything low-key and informal, part of which was to affect a mild cynicism, had built a kind of defensive carapace of low expectation about the event. Breaking through that shell, the collective emotion of the day crashed over us and swept us up in its warm tide. That was the very best thing.

— I dunno. I haven't really thought about it. The wedding's going to cost a lot, so maybe we shouldn't go too crazy, I replied.

— Right, we're only getting married, she said. — Anyway, I'll pay. What about the Caribbean?

— In the summer? That's where people go for winter breaks. What's wrong with Spain, or France. I don't fancy a long flight.

— The intrepid traveller.

— I tell you what. I wouldn't mind going back to Brittany. Do you remember I went there on a cycling holiday? And it's incredibly beautiful. Like Cornwall but with better weather and French food. Seafood too.

— Brittany? I'm not going on a cycling holiday for my honeymoon, you know.

— No, we could take the car on the ferry and tour around. But we could take our bikes on the roof-rack, I added.

— I am *not* spending my honeymoon on a cycling holiday, getting left behind while you pedal off into the distance.

— No, of course not. I just mean so we can potter about and explore without using the car all the time. You'd enjoy it.

A pause.

— Look, you don't have to bring your bike. But let me bring mine, OK? Just so that I can do the odd ride.

— So you can take off every day and leave me behind, you mean.

— No, it's our honeymoon. All I'm talking about is going out for a couple of hours in the early evening now and then – you know, like I did last summer when we went to Dorset with your family.

— I'd rather take my bike and do a few gentle rides together, she said.

— OK, great. Can I have the remote?

It was so difficult to come to terms with the idea of sacrificing that hard-earned edge of fitness. I had to force myself to accept that, with our wedding date set for the beginning of August, I should regard that as the end of my competitive season. My club championships were set for September, and ideally I would have wanted to maintain some form for the time-trial and hill-climb. But I had almost to take myself by the scruff of the neck and shake myself into the admission that, in reality, these were negligible goals. Still, though I knew how selfish the thought was, I struggled with it. When I tried on the pale linen suit I had bought specially for our wedding, my shaved legs felt strange inside the loose but cardboard-like texture of its trousers. With all my energy and desire so centred on cycling and perfecting myself in that, to re-direct myself towards another purpose entirely was like stepping off a moving train. But this was our wedding, I had to coach myself, and this was our honeymoon. There might be years of cycling ahead, but of these there would be only one.

There was so much to learn still. It was not just a question of tactics to be studied, but a whole, intricate system of values that the keen apprentice had to acquire. Invisible and unknown to outsiders, cycling possesses its own finely-wrought etiquette. The absolute command is of loyalty, even – should occasion require it – to the extent of sacrifice of the self. At its core, cycling is chivalric. It reminded me of a child's adaptation of the *Chanson de Roland* I had read long ago in school – of Roland's suicidal courage in holding off the barbarian hordes in order to save his king, the emperor Charlemagne. I had never realised how much the meaning of that tale had lodged with me, until I came to understand cycling's code of honour.

Fraternal loyalty to a teammate came first, requiring sacrifice or servitude as the occasion demanded. Clubmates tended to act as teammates, but some rode more tightly as squads than others. A well-drilled squad might attempt to organise a race, sending off one or two riders on an opportunistic early attack, and then defending their advantage by trying to break up any response from the bunch. But the purpose might be simply to soften up the bunch, to shake out some of the weaker riders.

If the race came back together, you would expect another attack immediately – and usually from their strongest rider, the unofficial team-leader. This, in a sense, was more a matter of team discipline than voluntary loyalty. But in any race, the unwritten law of cycling was that you should never do anything to compromise the racing advantage of a teammate, clubmate or friend.

The tactical paradox was that the circumstances of a race might turn opponents into temporary teammates. At the moment when the lead car sped off signalling the end of the race's neutralised zone, and again at the moment when each rider sprinted for the line, the race would become a pure competitive war of all against all. But in the intervening 30, 60, 80 or more miles all kinds of alliance might form: truces would be called, often simply on the strength of unspoken assumption, only to be broken further down the road. If you found yourself in a break, then every rider willing to work in that break became your ally. Only if the break was threatened, either by the gaining bunch or by the lack of its own cohesion, did it become permissible to attack the other riders and try to force a new selection or make a solo escape. In these situations a strange, unpredictable mixture of ruthless pragmatism and comradely solidarity would operate. Competition constantly mutated into cooperation and back again. A rider who ignored or traduced the rules of the game rode as a privateer who could expect no favours and no quarter from those who recognised him.

Riding a long race in Surrey one humid Sunday afternoon, I lost a bottle early during the first lap as my bike rattled over some broken road surface on a fast, twisting descent. I glimpsed behind to see the bottle skittering into the grass verge. There it lay, provoking me every lap, but to stop and retrieve it would have been unthinkable. To stop on that descent, dismount, pick up the bottle, remount and get up to speed again would have left me with a quarter-mile gap to bridge, I would have been lucky to get back on at all. The lucky ones had helpers to hand up extra bottles to them on the road circuit's main climb. Without that crucial bottle, I knew I would be struggling by the end.

The mishap left me with only one large bottle and a small one in my back pocket: just over a litre of water instead of two, on a hot, airless day when I might lose three or four litres in perspiration. Always after a summer race, I could scrape the dried salt from the side of my face and from my neck behind my ears. Like a cow licking a block of salt, I'd suck my fingers to get back a residue of the minerals I'd sweated out. To recover, I would drink until I felt bloated and nauseous. But it would often be hours before I could piss again; at first it came out a stinging dark yellow, concentrated by the dehydration.

I was going well that day. Despite a strong field, which contained several top amateurs and semi-pros, I even had a dig off the front myself for half a lap. I was riding well up the climb, staying in touch with the front as other riders were one by one winnowed out. But by the last lap, I was panting like a dog, practically hallucinating cold drinks. My legs felt heavy with the build-up of lactic acid. I knew that if I didn't get something to drink soon, to help flush the toxins from my taxed muscles, cramp would get me soon. As luck would have it, I had no teammates to call on that day. When the pace slowed for the last time up the main climb, in desperation I sought out Rob.

Rob Knight, the ex-pro who coached my club, still rode for a sponsored team, but he also kept membership of the VCL, his alma mater. Claiming a tenuous allegiance, I hoped to touch him for a drink from his bottle. He pulled a face to let me know I was taking a liberty, but let me take a swig from the bottle that I had just seen handed up to him.

I sucked greedily on the nozzle. It was Coca-Cola, warm, flat and sickly sweet. Coke was the last thing I wanted, but it slipped down my parched throat like John Mills's beer in *Ice Cold in Alex*.

— Hey, not all of it! That's enough.

Reluctantly, I handed it back. The liquid seemed only to tantalise, not slake my thirst. But I made it over the top of the hill with the bunch, now whittled down from more than sixty starters to less than twenty. It was maddening to know that dehydration was killing me. I knew I had good legs; if only I had had enough water, I could still have been in contention. As it was, I could only afford to ride steadily to survive to the line. Any intense effort and my legs were twitching, ready to seize in the agonising spasms of cramp.

On the back of the circuit, with three or four miles still to go, the attacks started going, with riders chipping off the front in ones and twos. Always relying on his speed in the final sprint, Rob at first ignored these moves, until the likelihood that he might miss the train altogether became impossible to ignore. I could only watch as he set off down the road on the back of a group of four chasers.

Soon I realised that all the remaining riders were as washed up as I was. Nobody came to the front to work, so there we were – watching the race ride away from us. Finding unbearable the thought that all my work earlier in the race was for nought, I came to the front of my rump of riders and pushed the pedals as hard as I dared. I saw Rob 200 metres down the road, sitting on the back of his group, turning once or twice to see if there were other riders coming up.

There was a short sharp climb just before the finishing

straight. The second I tried to get out of the saddle, my legs locked up. I had to creak up slowly while the remainder flitted past me. Down the other side, I could see that the race had come back together. Crippled with cramp, all I could do was roll towards the line and watch the bunch sprint up the road half a minute ahead of me.

Five minutes later, spinning slowly back to the race HQ to ease the acid out of the legs, Rob rode up alongside.

— You should never do that, you know.

— What?

— Chase down a teammate.

— But you're not my teammate, I said feebly.

— You'd taken some drink off me . . . it's the same thing. You don't chase a mate.

— You're right. Sorry.

— Well, you'll know next time, won't you?

After the wedding, Ruth and I spent the night at a smart country hotel. It looked exquisite, like a small stately home restored to glory. We parked up in our old, sun-faded red VW Polo. It was incongruous among the Jags, Porsches and Aston Martins sitting on their fat tyres. The gravel, almost carpet-like in its depth, crunched discreetly underfoot. We went straight up to our room to shower, rest and change before dinner. A porter carried our bags, and left politely before I could consider what the etiquette of tipping might be. Even the complimentary soaps were handmade, scented with herbs grown in the estate's own walled garden. Like Hunker and Munker, we were almost hysterically excited by so much luxury — surely not intended for us — and found ourselves giggling in complicity at each new wonder.

At dinner, there seemed as many waiters as diners. Glasses

were refilled before the level of liquor inside them had passed below halfway, while complex arrays of cutlery disappeared and reappeared with dazzling speed. Their French accents and extravagant *politesse* made us feel like unsophisticated sweethearts on a misjudged date. We were both too high and too exhausted to appreciate the food, which, like everything else, was rich and knowing. Instead, we compensated for our feelings of social inadequacy by playing a game of guessing the identities of fellow-guests. Ruth soon trumped my best efforts.

— They're dentists from Crawley, she whispered, meaning the pair of men in blazers with two very put-together women at a nearby table. Though a partner in this private mischief, I found myself shocked by this inverted snobbery, but titillated too. Her iconoclasm seemed brilliantly blasphemous and daring: to be so disgracefully *ungrateful* amid all this opulence! After all the distractions of the wedding, I was suddenly glad I had married this woman with the eyes and spirit of a Tartar.

We took breakfast in our room the next morning, rather than brave the dining room. We did not linger long, except for a short walk after breakfast that took in the walled gardens. No gardener could be seen working on the neatly organised plots of potatoes, curly kale and salad greens, the fruit bushes and herb beds of the large circular kitchen garden, nor on the billowing borders of lavender, shrubs and flowers in the formal garden; thus sustaining the illusion that the grounds cultivated themselves, as though in deference to the guests of the manor. When it was time to leave, I carried down our bags myself, feeling cheap but keen to forestall another awkward tipping moment. We presented ourselves to settle the bill, only to learn there was nothing to pay – my parents already had it covered. As we pulled away down the drive, we looked at one another and laughed. Our adventure as interlopers in luxury now over, it felt as though we had got off scot-free – like kids running away with pockets full of stolen apples. Boarding the ferry to St Malo the next day, among the middle-class holidaymakers, seemed securely familiar. After the great seduction of being the centre of attention, we were coming down.

Since I knew Britanny a little, I took charge of navigation. In practice, this meant taking a route which broadly reproduced the one Mick and I had taken on one of our cycling holidays with friends a few years earlier. This time there were things I had not bargained for. Roads that had seemed charming, picturesque or dramatic to cycle along, seemed to me now, as a motorist, merely roads – in other words, just dreary, empty time before we reached our destination. This was high season, too, and rooms were not so easy to come by. When we had been cycling, we could not have cared less about the quality of our accommodation. As long as there were beds and hot water, the cheaper the better. All that counted was to find an adequate restaurant in the evening, eat well and drink plenty, then stroll home in the dark knowing that sleep would come as soon as head hit pillow. A roll and café au lait the next morning and we would be on our way again. But now, on our honeymoon, the atmosphere and aspect of our overnight stays mattered very much.

On a cycling holiday, there is no such thing as a bad meal. You are so hungry when you sit down to eat that everything tastes good. The biggest problem was always finding something on the menu acceptable to the vegetarian in our group. Ruth and I discovered, though, that French provincial cooking had changed a good deal since Elizabeth David's day, and not necessarily for the better. A Muscadet in one place as acidic as it was overpriced; an *omelette aux champignons* with *champignons* that came from a can in another; then a trout that tasted as muddy as the water it had once, none too recently, swum in.

The mistake of revisiting scenes from my cycling holidays was that it made me look wistfully at every bend in the road, every arduous climb and long descent, and wish to be free on my bike with no more complex plan than to ride from village to village, seeing whatever I saw, with just a pair of panniers, a water-bottle and a map. It all cried out *cycle* to me. The fact that we had brought our bikes on this, our honeymoon, seemed a double folly. It wasn't as though Ruth really wanted to do much cycling, while for me the little that we did could never be enough. I found myself wishing that we had been in the Caribbean after all, lying on a brilliant sandy beach beside a topaz sea.

Few things are more dispiriting for a cyclist than puncturing. That sudden withdrawal of the privileges of the pneumatic tyre's magic-carpet ride deflates his mood as much as the inner tube.

A puncture might happen suddenly with a percussive report, or it might arrive by stealth. The first you would know of it then would be an unnerving woozy sensation, a partial loss of grip, as the tyre deformed under stress and smeared itself across the road as you cornered. But the commonest type of all was an impact puncture. A sharp blow, caused by hitting a pothole or large stone, would pinch the tyre and inner tube against each rim of the wheel, making two little slits in the tube. *Snakebites* we called them.

Impact punctures were invariably of the sudden and catastrophic type. Then, in an instant, before you'd even had time to touch the brakes or change direction, you would feel the metalled tarmac directly through the rigid alloy of your wheels. All that remained was to raise your hand to signal to other riders you were now merely a hazard for them to ride around. It felt like putting up your hand to take the blame for something. For a cyclist the physical sensation of riding on the rims is like chalk squeaking across a blackboard. But the hiss of escaping air was also the sound of lost illusions, the unforgiving feel of the road under your flat tyre a reminder of a harsh new reality. Every cyclist, anyone who's used a bike long enough to get a puncture, knows this feeling.

Picking up a *sharp* – a splinter of glass or shard-like piece of grit – was a random business. It could happen to anyone, at any time. You could go for months without mishap, and then have three punctures on a single ride. Sometimes you half-expected it on wet roads, and carried an extra inner in your back pocket. Rain might wash new grit across the road, but it also seemed that damp tyres picked up sharps more easily. Rear tyres punctured more often than fronts; the extra weight of the rider over the back wheel seemed to help a shard of glass or tiny arrowhead of flint work its way into the tyre's surface.

Some of the old boys who had been used to riding in the days when all racing bikes ran on *tubs* – tubular, one-piece tyres made from canvas and rubber that were glued onto the rim – used to have a sprung clip attached between the seat stays inside the rear brake calipers. This kept a wire armature pressing gently down onto the surface of their rear tyre as it rotated, in order to brush off sharps on the first revolution, before they were forced in deeper on the next. The development of fast, lightweight conventional tyres rendered such measures obsolete, since changing an inner tube was nowhere near so laborious as repairing a tub. Tubs were still standard on the track, where punctures were not a factor and their lightness and speed were at a premium. Compared to ordinary road tyres, track tubs seemed made of gossamer; for something so humble and utilitarian, almost feminine and pretty. The finest grade of all had walls of silk. A few purists preferred tubs for the road, but most of us had no time for the business of stitching and gluing them. There were tales of riders falling on long alpine descents because their rims had become so hot with friction from constant hard braking that the glue had melted, and tub and rim had parted company.

Even eschewing tubs, tyre choice was critical. When I first started competing, not in road-races but in time trials, I reasoned the narrower the tyre, the faster I would go. This was technically correct: a slim, slick tyre has less *rolling resistance* than a fatter one with tread. I picked the fastest tyre I could find: at 18mm, less than two-thirds of an inch across, it was narrower than the wheels themselves. I was nearing the end of my first time trial, out and back down a dreary section of the A20 at the eastern end of the North Downs on a raw, blustery Saturday morning in January, when I looked up from the road immediately ahead to survey the final climb. At that moment I ran through a sunken drain cover with a sickening twin jar, puncturing both front and rear tyres at once. I hobbled half a mile back to the changing rooms, wearing out the cleats on my shoes, wheeling my bike. On Monday I went out and bought a pair of 23s, and a new pair of cleats.

What seemed like misfortune was often inexperience. In a road-race, you learned to avoid riding in the gutter. There was more danger of getting *boxed in*, so that you could not respond to other riders' moves, and nowhere to go if something like a crash happened, but there was also more danger of puncturing. The road surface was always more likely to be broken at the side, the likelihood of picking up a sharp among the dust and grit greater. I even learned to swap tyres depending on conditions:

if the forecast was poor, I'd ride Michelins to get the extra grip from their softer compound; if the weather was fine, I'd run on Continentals (Contis were exceptionally hard-wearing and puncture-resistant).

If it was unexpectedly threatening rain right before a race, you would see the smarter riders fiddle with the valves on their wheels, let out a short hiss of air and then check the pressure by squeezing the tyre between finger and thumb. The idea was to give yourself just a little more margin by running on softer tyres than you normally would: releasing a little air would slightly increase the impression that each tyre would make on the road. This was a compromise judged by feel alone. You didn't want to run with too soft a tyre: too soft and there would be more rolling resistance. Too hard and you would sacrifice that vital extra grip.

Only in the wet did the absurdity of the bicycle's dynamics strike one: the fact of 75 kilos of rider and 10 kilos of bike staying upright round corners supported only by skinny pneumatic tyres – tyres that might provide an area of contact with the road no greater than a pair of thumb-prints. Suddenly, it seemed like a losing proposition. Improbable, impossible, more a matter of faith and magic than of scientifically verifiable laws of motion: a cyclist in the rain suffers a kind of existential doubt.

On a descent, especially, your eyes would be scanning the road surface ahead, watching for the longitudinal strips of smooth tar that are used to bond two sections of tarmac together. When wet, these strips became as treacherous as black ice. You had to look out not only for yourself, but for others. A rider more reckless or careless might make precisely the mistake you meant to avoid. If he fell in front of you, you might have nowhere to go but over his sliding prone form, and then you would be off yourself. A harsh pull on the brakes alone could do it. Not to brake is counter-intuitive, but the best riders keep their fingers off the levers and use their reflexes and roadcraft to thread a path through the flailing debris of fallen riders and bikes.

Hitting the tarmac at speed hurt. Whatever part of the body – shoulder, hip or butt – landed first felt as if it had been clubbed by an iron bar. Helmets had just become compulsory when I began racing. Before that, concussions had always been a risk: some riders wore padded skull caps, known as *hairnets*, but they offered minimal protection in a bad fall. The commonest injury was abrasions, *road rash*, but broken wrists and collarbones were an ever-present hazard.

The cold comfort of falling in the wet was that, like your bike, your body tended to skid on the road. You would still lose some skin, but the grazes would be more like burns through the polyester jersey or Lycra shorts, instead of the cheese-grater effect of a dry, dusty blacktop. Although the cold that came with rain suited my metabolism, I dreaded racing in the wet. The queasy, hollow-full feeling before a race that grew in your bowel and slowly rose towards your throat would be doubled when you knew there would be rain. You took your courage in both hands when you raced in the wet.

There was nothing you could do completely to avoid crashing but, in time, you used all your lore to avoid crashes. Sometimes everything would happen so instantaneously that it would be almost impossible afterwards to piece together how you had fallen and why. Questions of blame and responsibility were academic. The unspoken attitude of racers was that if you fell, it meant you were in the wrong place at the wrong time. Sympathy for fallers was in short supply.

Through the shock, you would be back on your cleated feet in a second, swearing and half-hopping, half-hobbling through the pain. As soon as you had mastered your pain, your next thought would be to remount and rejoin the race before losing contact with the back of the bunch. A frantic bike-check followed: spin the wheels to see if they were buckled; examine forks and frame for distortion or breakage; squint at the alignment of handlebars and brake hoods; ensure the chain was on, the rear derailleur intact . . . and off again. All too often, though, something would be bent or broken, and your race would be over.

It seemed so unjust. I would want to pick up my bike and hurl it in the hedge. You saw the pros do that on the Tour sometimes, when there had been a *chute* (how French, to have a word that makes an ugly accident sound like an elegant piece of choreography). A rider, caught up in a *chute*, might pick himself up and, though frantic to rejoin the race, discover a wheel buckled or forks bent. In disgust, he would throw the bike away. I could identify with that rage, though I would shudder at the way he treated the bike. A pro knew that his team car would pull up at any moment and a bustling mechanic would whisk a fresh machine from the roof-rack, hand it to the impatient rider and then give him a running push with a hand on the back of the saddle to launch him off down the road.

That was in the Tour. For us, mere mortals and amateurs, there was nothing to do but wait for a car to pick us up and return us to the race HQ, our cooling bodies already growing stiff from their fall. Then your chagrin at falling would be compounded by the bitter contemplation of expensive repairs you could ill-afford.

Like so much in cycling, I discovered, luck is a relative concept. To a great extent you made your own. But, for all your precautions and care, there would always be the unforeseen object that suddenly appeared at the very last instant between the wheels of the riders just feet in front of you — the rock in the road, or gaping pothole, or fallen bike, that had your name on it.

— *Ow!* Fuck, watch it! You're hurting me.

— Sorry, sorry. I'm doing it as gently as I can.

— You're enjoying this, aren't you? said Ruth, glaring at me over her shoulder. — You no-pain, no-gain pervert!

— Of course I'm not enjoying it.

I was not enjoying it. Needles made me feel as queasy as the next person; I was not in the habit of using them and I didn't much like anything about this — least of all inflicting the pain of deep, intra-muscular injection on Ruth. At the same time, I found it hard to keep a completely straight face about the procedure. Perhaps it was my embarrassment and discomfort that made me want to laugh it off, but there seemed an inherent absurdity in the situation. Ruth was lying on the bed on her front. Her knickers and tights were pulled down to her knees, reluctantly presenting the pale, round pillows of her buttocks to the syringe in my hand. A little pink flush gathered around the spot where the needle I'd just withdrawn broke the skin. I rubbed it briskly with a swab of cotton wool soaked in alcohol.

— There, I'm done. You just have to keep still is all. It's when you flinch that it hurts, I said. The truth was, at that moment, I felt in my veins a little rush of the power that doctors have.

— I don't think you'd find it so funny if it was me sticking a needle in your arse and pumping you full of hormones. It's just a game to you.

— Look, am I laughing? I protested, suppressing a smile nonetheless. — You're right: I'd hate my body to be messed about with like this. But it just *is* the price of getting pregnant. And if you do get pregnant, then your body will be a maelstrom of crazy hormones anyway.

— Yeah great. I can't wait, sighed Ruth, pulling up her tights and straightening out the black mini-skirt, her favourite.

You could race for an hour, maybe more, and feel strong. But if you had neglected to eat and drink, you would hit a wall. *Bonking; getting the bonk*, or *the knock*. It meant a crisis of dehydration and a crashing blood-sugar level. If you got it badly, you would feel weak, all your strength suddenly gone. Your heart would flutter and palpitate. You would break out in a cold sweat. You might feel stupid or confused, lightheaded like a sub-aqua diver suffering from nitrogen narcosis. In the worst case, your vision might go dark and tunnel-like. Then it felt like a premonition of death. If you reached that state in a race, it would be too late: by the time your body could use the food and drink you gulped down in desperation to recover, the race would have left you far behind. It was simple: the body is an internal combustion engine, and engines run on fuel. Getting the bonk was like running out of petrol.

Little and often, little and often — that was the rule. To use a momentary lull in the action to pull a banana from a lumbar pocket. Cycling jerseys have a back-to-front look with pouches that sit on your kidneys as you ride. Bananas are easiest to chew and chug down when you're breathing hard through your mouth. Cereal bars or flapjacks have the right content but the wrong texture. They turn into a claggy, choking lump, stuck to your cheek like a wad of tobacco. Fine for a club run, but too hard to eat in a race. Easy to swallow, bananas were also easy on the stomach. Sometimes, in a race, you could ride so hard, it felt as though you were twisting your guts for every last ounce of effort. The demands you placed on your body, pulling the blood away from every quarter but the legs that were driving you, could disrupt even your digestion – make you retch or give you diarrhoea.

Carbohydrate drinks were just coming in. At first unflavoured – starchy, slightly sugary with a hint of maltiness – they were unappetising but effective. I learnt to add a pinch of salt to the mix in the bottle, or better still to mix an electrolytic supplement like Gatorade with the carbohydrate drink. The stomach absorbs isotonic liquid more efficiently than plain water. Losing salts led to cramps. Bananas, again, were good; they contain potassium. Boxers drink grapefruit juice for the same reason. Some riders never seemed to suffer with cramp; for me, it could be a race finisher. Calves, quads, even hams, locked solid with lactic acid and salt deficit.

Even if I had survived the race without trouble, cramp might still strike hours later. I would wake up in bed at night, after a race, shooting out a leg in an involuntary effort to stop my hamstring seizing solid. The bigger the muscle, the greater the pain. At other times I'd lie on the sofa, relaxing in a pair of shorts, fascinated by the tiny spasms rippling over the smooth-shaved surface of my calves, like the aftershocks of an earthquake.

I never knew anyone who used drugs. Possibly some riders used the Creatine supplements you could buy in health food stores, but if they did, they kept quiet about it. Only one talented young racer I knew, who had been to France to try out with a top amateur club (the traditional route to a professional career on the Continent), returned with tales of rife drug use. 'They're all at it,' he said, his own dream swept away. Even the amateurs? 'All of them. Everybody else is doing it, so if they want to get on, they've got to do it too.' And if that was at amateur level, then what could be inferred about the professional scene was too obvious to merit comment. Let us simply say that the successive scandals from the 1998 Tour onwards contained few surprises for anyone who knew racing: the rumours, about who was on what, had been bumping around for several seasons.

What kept it quiet for too long was, in effect, a conspiracy in which every party hid its head in the sand – the governing body, the race organisers, the sponsors, the press, the team managers, even the riders themselves – while the doctors got on with the dirty job of pumping riders full of designer steroids, EPO, human growth hormone and who knows what else. The journalists refused to rock the boat because they knew their livelihood would be finished if they were never granted another interview with the stars of the sport. But what was most distressing was the attitude of the riders: with very few exceptions, they closed ranks and lied consistently; they seemed to have no thought about the long-term consequences for their own health, and certainly no sense of an ideal of drug-free purity in cycling; even when caught, they were beyond shameless – they seemed indignant that anyone might dare to suggest they should not cheat. They simply wanted the pharmaceutical fix they'd become accustomed to, and without which they knew their results would suffer. As Jacques Anquetil, five-times winner and chilly aristocrat of the Tour, had once famously remarked during an earlier episode of its cyclical drugs scandals, did anyone seriously expect them to ride the Tour 'on mineral water alone'?

I read Paul Kimmage's *A Rough Ride* while I was still racing. Though shocked by his disillusioning portrait of professional racing life in the early eighties, in time his and others' accounts of riders rustling in their backpockets to find a syringe or a foil-wrapped portion of whizz came to seem almost quaint. If you were not careful, you could almost catch yourself feeling nostalgic for the good-old, bad-old days – at least compared with the medically-sanctioned, industrialised system of doping that had taken hold of pro cycling in the 1990s.

Although we had got as far as the IVF procedure, the prospect of pregnancy still seemed theoretical. At first, we had been told that we could join an NHS waiting list for IVF that was long enough to ensure that our (non-existent) children might just possibly receive help conceiving our grandchildren. At that point, out of a mixture of old-fashioned ideological aversion to private medicine and plain parsimony, neither of us had been inclined to pay for private treatment. Then the hospital had received a wedge of research funding for their fertility treatment programme. Overnight, there was no waiting list.

Neither of us paused to think further. Having arrived at that point, it was as though the momentum of our desires had acquired the force of destiny. If IVF was being offered free, then, of course, IVF we would do. If we felt uneasy, we took refuge behind our shared scepticism. The Assisted Conception Unit's statistics gave us no better than a seven-to-one shot. The likelihood of disappointment did not encourage one to consider the consequences of successful treatment.

Treatment. The procedure, which had me administering daily injections for a fortnight, had a 'do-it-yourself' amateurishness that made me think it couldn't possibly work. Before that, Ruth had been required to use a nasal spray.

— Have you snorted today? I would ask her. I was supposed to remind her, but it was impossible not to turn it into a joke.

It felt unreal, this grown-up game of doctors and nurses,

and it did have a lame comic quality, like a clumsy parody of recreational drug-taking – one last binge before the responsibilities of pregnancy and parenthood. The nasal spray was to switch off Ruth's own hormones; then the injections would take endocrinological control, ensuring a rich harvest of eggs on the follicles of her ovaries. In IVF, ripeness is all.

Ruth grumbled about the injections. I was sympathetic, because who likes injections, after all? Although it was chiefly to keep costs down, no doubt someone at the ACU had thought there was a psychological benefit in including the treated woman's partner in the IVF procedure. The fact that his role seemed a mildly sadistic one, with an unfortunate symbolism, seemed to have escaped them.

I could understand Ruth's distaste for her body being fooled around with. Secretly, I was grateful it was not me. Cycle-racing had given me a heightened sense of physical purity. I felt I belonged to an elite. I was fitter than I had ever been in my life, fitter than anyone I knew besides a few fellow-racers. Submitting to the type of treatment Ruth underwent involved surgical procedures and powerful hormone-controlling drugs that, to me, would have been an affront to this purity. The classical ideal of human perfectibility, which Leni Reifenstahl had hymned in her paean to athletic endeavour, *Olympia*, had a palpable reality for me also.

I once spoke to a veteran Channel swimmer who explained how he had had to learn to swim through the exhaustion, cold, nausea and sheer pain of hour after hour in the open sea. I had just swum two miles in open water. The water was flat calm and 70°. The swim had taken me an hour: it was taxing, but not horribly so, yet I knew that it was near enough the limit of my capabilities. How someone could swim in the high sea, in a swell, against tides, and spend 16 hours or more in water in the low 60°s to cover the 20-mile Strait of Dover, was beyond my imagination.

Defeat can be only in the mind, the Channel swimmer insisted, because there is nothing the body will not do, given the will to drive it. *The body is a beautiful machine*, he said, gazing away into the hazy distance. He sounded like a proud mechanic admiring an old Bugatti or Bentley. But I knew exactly what he meant. Cycling had taught me to think of my body as a machine.

In all sporting disciplines, there is a necessary self-regard and focus that excludes all else. It begins with a practical preoccupation with the body, how it works and what, from minute to minute, it is communicating; but in time it comes to acquire a free-standing aesthetic dimension. The body is a beautiful machine but, like all machines, it requires maintenance and working on. The narcissism of athletes arises, then, because athletes must become engineers of themselves. For the cyclist, his legs, satin-smooth, oiled and gleaming, are as integral to this idea of speed and performance as the polished chrome and alloy of his bike.

If he did not belong to a heavily sponsored team, the cyclist had to be his own *soigneur*, his own care-taker. After a race, for instance, I would clean off my grime-soiled legs with an alcohol-based antiseptic spray, apply ointment to their shaved surfaces and gently massage away the toxins in my muscles. Even among amateurs, this elaborate ritual of tenderness towards oneself was commonplace. The athletic body is something that a man creates, produces from within himself, through sacrifice and pain, with love and care. His body, you might say, is his baby.

*　　*　　*

We were waiting at the clinic. Once more, we sat opposite the pinboard covered with snaps of babies and toddlers sent in by grateful parents. Its smugness annoyed me all over again – the bland assurance of those who believed their little bundle was a miracle they had somehow deserved, as opposed to what in reality it was: a lucky ticket in a biological lottery. But mainly I was bored, sitting in this corridor where we seemed to spend increasingly large portions of our time. I thought instead about the upcoming weekend's race, seeing the circuit in my head, visualising a scenario of how I might slip the bunch and get away.

— What are you going to do if we get pregnant? Ruth interrupted my reverie.

— How do you mean?

— I mean, do you intend to change your life? she elaborated slowly and evenly as though I were slightly stupid. Which in a sense I was because, amid all the process of IVF, the idea of becoming a parent seemed to grow more remote than ever, scarcely having consequences worth contemplating.

— Will you give up cycling?

Her left hand brushed the top of my thigh, where my leg was exposed below the shorts I was wearing. She stroked upwards, against the grain of the stubble, and then withdrew her hand suddenly, as if stung by nettles.

— Yes, I suppose I will ... when I need to, I replied uncertainly. — I mean, I wouldn't have to give up right away, would I? There'd be no point in stopping cycling simply while you're pregnant. I'd give up a couple of weeks before your due date. That would be OK, wouldn't it?

Ruth said nothing for a moment.

— And after the birth you'd give up?

— Yes, sure. I mean, I *was* hoping I could still get out

and do the odd ride at weekends, I said, seeing at last that she was not simply teasing me, but asking for some kind of reassurance. — But there's no way I could race, obviously.

— It's just that I don't think you've thought about what it would mean as a commitment, said Ruth.

I find myself bridling at the word *commitment*. Why was this under question now? *I am here, aren't I?* I wanted to say. But parenthood as a goal seemed almost as distant as a comfortable retirement. And like a pension, it was something I subscribed to, but only because it seemed like a good idea in the abstract. It had no reality for me in the here and now.

Then, in an instant, I saw that for Ruth it was suddenly very real. She was minutes away from having two tiny amoebas, each just a few cells across, implanted in her womb. Two little embryos, potential future human beings. For her, pregnancy began here.

It was true that I had not thought much about the sacrifices I would need to make. There were a handful of cyclists I knew whom I would see, half-undressed after a race, holding a baby as if it were another kind of trophy. Their wives or girlfriends came to the races and turned a corner of the village hall into a makeshift crèche. These cyclists tended to be the sponsored riders who won the races, on the cusp perhaps of getting a contract and going pro. How else, I supposed, could they justify the commitment of time and energy to their cycling?

Men like Mick and I were only a click or two below them in ability, but we were older. We were hitting thirty. Physically we were at the peak of our potential, but we had little prospect of improving much further, and definitely no ambition for a career in cycling. For us, cycling was many things beside a sport – a passion, a fraternity, a way of life almost – but it was not a living. Neither of us lived with women who would resign themselves to spending their Sundays hanging around draughty church halls and dodging spring showers to stand at the roadside, holding the baby while Daddy made laborious circuits of the Surrey countryside. We had a life beyond cycling.

Now, though, that life was demanding that choices be made. Whatever might happen, I had a delay before any real adjustment would be required of me. Ruth, on the other hand, felt the full vertigo of our decision. Everything that had made her what she was – childhood, adolescence and young adulthood – was now to be put behind her. Pregnancy would mark the process of becoming a different kind of woman, a woman like her own mother and her mother's mother before that. It was as though she were seeing her own reflection in facing mirrors, the line receding behind her, seeming to beckon. There was, after all, to be a reckoning with the biological destiny against which she had always felt herself in rebellion. It required her to step into the dark unknown, a void which threatened to be as fatally irrevocable as a hangman's drop. She needed to know that I would be there, holding her hand, as we took that step.

I struggled to imagine what it must be like for her, but my imagination stumbled. The challenges I set for myself in cycling were circumscribed and artificial; this was *real*. I liked to think that I had learned things worth knowing about myself and about life from bike-racing – a cluster of values with loyalty at its heart, a self-confidence and self-reliance that in some ways I lacked before, and the sense of having a place in the world – but this was where the metaphor broke down. Cycling was just cycling; this was life. There were things that did not translate. I felt reluctant about giving up something as trivial as shaving my legs, yet Ruth was about to experience an alteration to her sense of physical integrity, a loss of personal autonomy, more absolute than I could even bring myself fully to comprehend. The idea of sacrificing my precious fitness was almost unbearable to me; she was committing her whole self, body and soul, to the process of creating a new, and other, person.

— You're right, I suppose, I replied quietly, trying simultaneously to keep our conversation private and not to sound defensive. — It's just that it's pretty abstract for me still.

She looked at me enquiringly, but didn't respond. It occurred to me then that I had not wanted to think carefully about the possibility of becoming a parent because I had not wanted to raise my own expectations – only to have to deal with the likely failure of IVF. The fact that it had only just occurred to me somehow called into question its authenticity.

— But you know I'm committed. I would never put anything else ahead of this. I'm here.

Ruth nodded. Was this enough? She had had a pre-med some minutes earlier. She seemed to go inside herself.

— Good luck, honey. She stared back at me as if I'd said something incomprehensible.

By Christmas, Ruth was pregnant. A few weeks after that, we learnt that she was expecting twins. It was a possible consequence of IVF that we had hardly considered; if we'd wanted, we could have had three embryos put back, in which case it might have been triplets. Without the faintest idea what a twin birth would mean, we felt delighted with our luck. But it meant a more arduous pregnancy ahead for Ruth. The tiredness and the morning sickness began almost immediately. That the sickness was bad was a good sign, she said bravely. It meant the hormones were strong; it meant she would keep the babies.

The sickness lasted beyond the end of March, into April.

There were days in the dark turn of that year when the first sound I would hear in the mornings would be Ruth being sick in the toilet. Then she would force herself to eat, some toast perhaps and weak tea, and set off for work, having barely exchanged a word. Sometimes I would call her later at work, ask how she was. Sick, she'd say. As though I really needed to ask. Work at least distracted her from the nausea. But then my calls came like an unwelcome reminder, and she would break off abruptly.

In the evening I would cook as usual, but often she complained about the smell and did not eat with me. Garlic was banned; I tried to think of plain, bland meals. But my breath was tainted all the same, perhaps from what I had eaten earlier in the day. It stank of garlic, wine or coffee. Besides suffering from nausea, she was always tired; she had nothing left after work. By the time I had cleared up and watched the news, she was in bed asleep.

Weeks passed in this routine. It was hard to know what to say or do to help. There was nothing, except be there.

— Do you know what it feels like? She asked. — It feels like I've been taken over by aliens. There are these two little aliens inside me, hoovering up everything they need at my expense.

Feeling useless, I suggested that I pack in cycling sooner than promised. The half-heartedness of this offer must have been apparent; Ruth shook her head. She knew I wouldn't help by moping around, wishing I were elsewhere.

Instead, knowing that this was to be my last season and a brief one at that, I pitched myself into training with more single-minded determination than ever. Sometimes the schedule became so tight that I would get up on a weekday morning when it was still dark, to fit in a training ride before work.

144

The thought of another man might have been: how will I provide for my coming family? More conscious than before of the need to earn, I was busy at work. But I wanted my racing, too, and now I was racing against time.

Over the Easter weekend I took part in the Tour of Ulster, a three-day stage race through the hills around Enniskillen. Mick and I were riding as part of a team for the South London division of the British Cycling Federation. We wore jerseys I had never seen before, pure white with a red cross and a blue wavy symbol which looked like the Thames Water logo. The jersey was pretty, and it felt thrilling to be united with riders from other clubs in a single team, but we were nervous about how the Flag of St George might be perceived in Northern Ireland.

After a poor first day, our team showed well. On the final day, in a stage that began in driving rain, two of us made a break of five that stayed away for 40 miles. We made the line a matter of seconds before the remnants of the chasing bunch charged home. And given that we were two in a break of five, we should have been able to work out some tactical move at the finish that would have given my teammate at least a shot at the sprint. But, as usual, I had nothing left for the gallop; I was not even thinking clearly, unable to focus on much besides getting over the line. I ended up with fourth; he with third. But that placing, and a decent time in the previous day's time-trial stage, put me in the top ten. It had been an epic escape, one that later became etched in the memory, in a vivid series of sights and sensations, as a highlight of my cycling career. Then, though, all I knew was that I had some great form; I was determined to make the most of it before the summer was up. My plan was that I would race until the end of June, my season ending a safe four weeks before Ruth was due.

We planned to catch the ferry from Belfast that evening. Leg-sore from the long weekend's racing, we ambled around the departure building, spending our change at the kiosk on Mars bars and flapjacks as our bodies remembered their calorie deficit. We drove back through the night in shifts, the others dozing as they could. The outskirts of London came up at first light. We were all tired, thinking about having to get straight to work on not enough sleep. The goodbyes in the cold grey light and damp air of the city were perfunctory. My bike was still filthy from the previous day's race in the rain, and a couple of spokes in the back wheel were broken. This return to civilian life, this end of the adventure, was a melancholy moment. It was the way you feel when you reach the end of a novel you have loved, when you can hardly bear to be parted from its world and be landed back in your own quotidian reality.

A month later, at the beginning of May, Ruth and I took a fortnight's holiday on a Greek island with my parents. In her fifth month, Ruth was already heavily pregnant; still, we hired bikes anyway to get around the island. The road through the centre of the island rose in a gentle incline. It was scarcely steep enough to freewheel down in the morning, but in the late afternoon Ruth laboured up it, panting in the hot, dry air.

I would pedal beside her, pushing with one hand on the small of her back, as you might occasionally see a clubmate help someone who was struggling on a climb. It was surprising, when you took this help, how much difference it made. I had not taken a push for several seasons – it was a matter of pride. And because it was a matter of pride, you had to be sure it would be welcome to the other rider when you gave it. Many would rather suffer alone than feel humiliated by accepting a push.

— You like this, don't you? Ruth said. — It means you're getting more exercise.

I didn't deny it. Once or twice I took my creaky bike with its loose saddle up the winding mountain road to the highest peak of the island, a bleak grey outcrop that jutted out like a boxer's chin towards the Turkish mainland a few miles away. The goats could go as they pleased but I could not approach the summit because a sentry post and an official sign indicated that I would be trespassing on a military installation. A quarter of a mile ahead, on the cliff's edge, a concrete bunker bristling with antennae maintained its vigil over an eastern Aegean the colour of copper sulphate and, in the hazy distance beyond, the mountainous coast of Asia Minor.

In the evening, after our meal, we would freewheel home almost noiselessly except for the gentle hiss of our tyres in the dust of the track down to our little villa. Once, on this ride home, we surprised a nocturnal bird on the road. It was a scops owl, a diminutive member of the owl family whose cry you often hear on those islands punctuating the passing hours of the night with a sound unnaturally like an intermittent electronic alarm. We spent the days on the beach. The best and most secluded of these demanded a strenuous walk around several craggy headlands, along goat tracks lined with pungent thyme and oregano, parched sage and thorny little bushes that looked like low, grey gorse. Our shins and ankles were soon criss-crossed with scores of little cuts. Even in May, by late morning, the sunlight and heat could be harsh. Away from the villages, the landscape resembled a biblical wilderness, with barely a shrub to provide shade, just the occasional tumbledown shack of a goatherd or abandoned farmer's cottage.

— Do you realise what it's like? Ruth asked as we paused

to rest on one of these walks. — It's like carrying a huge hot-water bottle strapped on to you the whole time.

We would rest every half-mile or so while she regained her breath and sipped from a water bottle. She sipped, and walked, and stopped, and sipped.

The heat continued after we came home: 1995 was a long hot summer. I know the year because it was when our children were born. After our holiday, the form I had had in Ireland seemed to have evaporated. Two weeks had been long enough to lose the edge I had gained. They greeted my tan with ironic whistles in the changing room, but I struggled the next time I raced. I was off the pace. Other riders had picked up while I was away. They went better in the warm conditions, while I suffered. As the weeks went by towards the date I had set for my last race, I found my motivation waning. Mick, too, had scaled down racing to plan for his own forthcoming wedding. My last race came and went without leaving a trace on my memory. I slipped, with something like relief, into indolent preparations for the arrival of our twins: shopping for some baby vests, some socks, a pair of cotton hats; assembling the wooden cot, which seemed improbably vast even for the pair of them.

Ruth went into labour just before a weekend in the middle of August. The atmosphere was so sultry I was sweating just sitting still. I sweated easily; I sweated all the time. When you're fit, you sweat more. I had only to move and the perspiration would bubble up like a hundred tiny springs from my brow. As she laboured, Ruth sweated too. I mopped her forehead and temples with a damp flannel. From time to time I would refresh it at the basin in the corner with its strange hospital taps. However long I left on the tap, the water never ran cold enough.

A soft-voiced young obstetrician consulted with Ruth. He noticed my legs, and asked:

— You're a cyclist? He was Irish, from the Republic.

— Yes, I replied, delighted. — You too?

He was, or had been, a little. Perhaps he was merely being modest, but in Ireland, even a little meant a lot. It was more like the Continent there; they understood cycling. Riders like Sean Kelly and Stephen Roche had been national heroes. It is part of the popular psyche there, not the strange, marginal sport it is here.

Suddenly, I felt self-conscious to be talking about cycling in front of Ruth. It was her consultation, and she was in labour. Perhaps the obstetrician felt the faint impropriety, too, and the conversation, as soon joined, dried up. He re-addressed himself to Ruth in his calm manner.

— He seemed nice, I whispered to Ruth, after he had left. — I hope we get to keep him.

Her eyes closed, Ruth shrugged. Which I took to mean that either it was a matter of indifference or she did not count on it.

She was correct. It was another 36 hours before the twins were delivered. We never saw our Irish obstetrician again. By the time his next rotation would have been due, we were long gone – reassigned to the maternity ward and a whole new world.

Weeping with exhaustion, Ruth was given a late epidural. Baby 1 was engaged but was not moving down. Both babies' heartbeats were monitored. Finally, on the Sunday morning, with mounting anxiety about Baby 1's possible distress, Ruth was wheeled into theatre for a caesarian. Huddling behind the curtain the surgical staff raised over her stomach, Ruth's sister and I held her hands and sang nursery rhymes, whatever came into our heads, to comfort Ruth as the surgeons opened up her abdomen and rummaged around inside.

Time slowed down and then speeded up. There seemed to be too many people in the room, and suddenly two blood-specked packages – Baby 1 and Baby 2 – were being passed around and fussed over in resusciteurs. In a matter of moments, it seemed, the room cleared and Ruth's sister and I were both holding babies swaddled in cotton gauze blankets for Ruth to see. We had to hold them almost in her face since she was still prostrate on a gurney, immobilised by the epidural, almost too dazed with drugs, emotion and weariness to respond.

Our new lives had begun.

Stage 6

As usually happens in everyone's life, there are some events for which we cannot precisely trace the cause. Similarly, while riding a Bicycle, the Chain can accidentally get off, the Tyres may get punctured and rarely, of course, the Fork may break. These incidents signify the jerks and jolts in life.

— R. N. Khurana

Good Friday, a little more than 18 months later. It was not cold, but it was overcast and threatening rain. As if by tradition, the Easter Meeting at the Herne Hill Stadium always seemed narrowly to escape foul April weather. Several hundred could be relied upon to show up despite blustery conditions, creating an incongruous crowd in that genteel, leafy London suburb.

They would come in cars, on foot and, of course, by bike. Drawn to watch their friends and clubmates race on the same circuit and on the same afternoon as the big-name international sprinters and pursuiters, they cheerfully paid the entrance fee at the gate. The star sprinters would top the bill – massively developed athletes like the former East German Michael Hübner and the American Marty Nothstein – men whose calf muscles alone were as thick as an ordinary racer's thighs.

The Good Friday Meet was by far the biggest event in the stadium's calendar. It might be a pale imitation of the bierfest bonhomie of the great Six Day Races that take place every year in Ghent and other Dutch and German cities, and a mere ghost of the great gladiatorial contests of cycling that once graced Paris's Vel d'hiv and Madison Square Gardens in New York, but this half-concealed little corner of South London's cycling history has always contrived to foster its own particular atmosphere of restrained carnival.

So distracted were we that year – and not only by the frantic pattern of life as working parents – the bank holiday came upon us in a hurry. We had made no plans for the Friday. I was surprised all the same when Ruth readily agreed to my suggestion of making an outing to Herne Hill to watch the races. I was even more surprised that she agreed we could cycle over to the track. I knew there would be many of my racing pals there, and for the minority that had children it would be something of a family affair. Some I had not seen since the twins were born. We did not usually go so far afield with the children in the tow-trailer that we used for the three-quarter-mile journey to their nursery. But for old time's sake, I liked the idea of arriving by bike.

— Are you sure? I checked. — I don't mind driving.

— No. It's OK. We can go by bike, as long as you pull the trailer.

It was hard to read Ruth's passive acquiescence with my wishes. It made me uneasy and, for some indefinable reason, a little depressed. She knew me very well. How, on the one hand, I liked to please – liked to think of myself as obliging and relaxed. But also how stubborn I could be once my heart was set on something. It was possible, I felt, that right then she did not have the will to propose an alternative, nor the energy to argue the issue. It left me half-grateful, half-guilty, for her compliance.

I bundled the children into the trailer and put their helmets on, taking care to put their little coats in after them. Joe wanted to be held and protested about being strapped in until he found his thumb. I said something emollient and zipped the flap. The trailer's nylon covering had clear plastic windows on the sides and in front, to give them some kind of view as I pedalled, and to allow me to glance back at them.

Once Ruth had locked the front door, our odd little convoy got underway. Out of habit I wore my helmet; Ruth wore none. It flattened her hair and ruined the curls, she used to say, and anyway she didn't ride fast enough to need a helmet. Sometimes I had argued otherwise, and once – after she was knocked off by a car (though luckily unhurt) – prevailed for a few weeks. That day I said nothing. Ruth had cancer. There were no long ringlets to flatten any more; the chemo had seen to that. Our hopes of remission were slipping away with every day that passed. So what, compared to that, could one usefully say about the prognosis for someone who rode a bicycle without a helmet? I glanced up at the lowering sky and chose to worry instead about whether it would rain.

We wound our way slowly through the back streets of south London, heading for Herne Hill by the most cycle-friendly route I could find. Ruth rode behind me, vaguely shielding the trailer from following traffic. There was no way of reaching Herne Hill by any direct means without negotiating a hill. My route took us up to Dog Kennel Hill behind Camberwell, just a short spin from Denmark Hill and King's Hospital where the children had been born.

With the trailer to tow, I put my bike in a small gear and took the short climb as easy as I could. Halfway up the hill, pedalling gently, I looked round. Unable to keep up, Ruth had dropped back. Turning my smallest gear, I slowed almost to walking pace. But it was no good. Ruth could not catch up. As long as I was sensible, we had always been able to ride around town together comfortably. And here I was pulling the trailer.

— Do you want to stop? I called back.

— No.

— Do you want to rest?

Ruth shook her head.

— No, go on. I'll catch up.

She still did not look sick. She had been sick during the chemo, very sick. But that was the chemo, not the cancer. She had mentioned a day or two ago that she was feeling breathless. I had taken in what she'd said, but had not stopped to think what it might mean. With cancer, you exist with this constant double-think: you fear the worst, but choose to believe the best. We decided to discount the breathlessness, which was pretty mild, she said, as a side-effect of radiotherapy.

On this Good Friday, the worst would not be denied. Ruth's deterioration was right in front of us. Neither of us needed to say anything; what we were both thinking was *lung cancer*. I could not now escape the bitter irony of our outing, the outing we were making at my behest. We were on our way to watch some of the fittest, fastest men in the world on two wheels – men with vast lungs, acres of healthy, life-giving tissue – and my wife was gradually dying, robbed of breath.

I felt myself crumple inside. I wanted to pull over and sit on the kerbstone with my head in my hands and wish it all away.

Instead, I did as she said. I turned away and carried on pedalling slowly up the hill. From time to time I would look over my shoulder to check that Ruth was not lost too far behind.

No hill ever hurt me more.

* * *

154

Ten minutes later, we arrived at the stadium. Neither of us said anything about what had happened on Dog Kennel Hill. There was nothing to say.

We locked up our bikes and, picking up a child each, made a slow tour around the track perimeter. The banked-up bends afforded a good view over the whole circuit, so other than the grandstand of the clubhouse, the banking was where most of the spectators were congregated. In a manner typical of track-racing, intense flurries of action would be followed by frequent tedious intermissions. Over the PA, an announcer kept up a desultory burble of results from the heats and lists of the line-up for forthcoming races. Competitors could be seen in front of the clubhouse, riding on rollers to keep their legs warm and supple. From a distance, it made a faintly surreal sight. They could sit up to chat with bystanders, all the while pedalling away but going nowhere.

Just then, with a shock of revelation, the sun at last broke through the dense grey cloud. Unexpectedly illuminated, the scene acquired garish colour. The white surface of the track shone like a snow-covered ski piste. The riders in their team jerseys took on the unmixed palette of a Léger painting. The grass of the football pitch which filled the middle of the circuit glowed an unreal, algae-green.

— Hey, Matt! How're you doing?

A tall, lanky fellow, with hair receding like mine only more so, was smiling at me. He wore glasses and a trim goatee. I knew him but I couldn't remember his name. It had been a while, after all. He was a New Zealander, I recalled, a gentle, earnest guy whom I knew only from club-runs, not from racing. Too late I realised how little I really wished to meet or talk to anyone from this old life. What a labour it suddenly seemed – the repeated narrations of the intervening time, the dreary getting-up-to-date, and now the sober admission of our official status as family-with-cancer-victim.

— Fine! How are you? I asked, hale enough, I hoped, to cover my embarrassment at forgetting his name. I fudged the introductions.

— This is Ruth. And this is Joe . . . and this is Lola.

— I'm Steve, he said, offering his hand to Ruth. It was plain he wanted the encounter enough to overlook my gaffe.

— And this is Susan . . . and our son, Ethan, he said, indicating a woman with short blonde hair, an open face and, riding on her hip, a small brown-eyed boy who looked very much like his dad except for the goatee. I smiled hello at her and said a little 'Hi' to Ethan, which was enough to make him tuck his face into his mother's fleece.

— So, you getting out much? Steve asked. He meant on the bike, of course.

— Nah, not much. I get out for a couple of hours on a Saturday morning if I can, but that's about it. You know, work, kids . . .

He nodded in recognition. On impulse, and to get it over with, I added:

— Plus Ruth's been unwell. It's all more difficult.

I glanced at Ruth to see whether she was annoyed by my candour, but her features remained a mask of impassivity. She seemed somewhere else.

— Yeah, I'm really sorry. We heard . . . from Mick, he added so that it didn't seem so much like gossip.

Now I saw. If I were him, I would have been dreading this meeting, but equally he would have felt too bad if he had let us go by with a nod and a wave. He was just a decent person being decent. Nevertheless his decency made it incumbent upon us to accept his concern and compassion with good grace. We were learning this new etiquette that applies to the charmed circle of the cancer patient.

— Where have you been getting treatment? Susan asked Ruth, a little too brightly.

— At Guy's, Ruth replied, shifting in order to hike Joe up on her hip.

— Of course, said Susan knowingly.

— Susan works at St Thomas's, Steve put in by way of explanation.

— So what do you do there? I asked.

— I'm a counsellor, she explained. — We see a lot of oncology patients.

So much more hygienic than handling people with cancer, the uncharitable thought flashed up in my brain.

— Oh, so you must know Lorri M———. I hazarded the one name I knew from the Guy's and Tommy's psych services.

Her face fell sharply at the name, as if the sun had passed behind a cloud.

— Er, yes ... she's my boss in fact, came the guarded reply.

— Susan and her boss ... they don't get on very well, elucidated Steve unnecessarily to me in aside.

— Oh, I said. I was curious, of course. Without wishing this person I'd known for a minute and a half any specific malice, I found myself wishing to seize on the moment. To probe her discomfort further and savour its tang. *What is the matter with me?* I thought. I used to be a nice person.

By a narrow margin, better instincts triumphed; the subject was dropped.

— Did you just get here? Steve enquired, starting over.

— Yeah, about ten minutes ago. What have we missed?

— We saw Hübner warming up when we got here. Jeez, the legs on that guy!

— When's he on?

— Oh, they save the best till last. After the points race and the pursuit.

— Oh, so we get to see Obree on his home-made bike first?

— Should be something. I don't know how he holds that position of his.

— Right, how can he breathe properly? I said without thinking.

I looked over and was relieved to see Susan and Ruth engaged in some sort of conversation about nurseries. The next minute they were calling riders to the line, and I caught Ruth's eye. Saying we meant to complete a tour of the circuit, we made our excuses.

I remember nothing about the racing that afternoon. What I recall is that it turned out hot and Joe was miserable. He could only temporarily be distracted by the bright colours and spectacle of all the cyclists. Mostly he was clinging and unhappy.

As we sat on the bleachers, squinting into the unseasonal sunshine, it finally became clear why: without warning he was sick on the planking at our feet. Fortunately, the seating in that part of the stand was half empty. The people nearby politely ignored us as we used up a week's worth of wetwipes cleaning him up and hastily smeared away the worst of his vomit under the scaffolding.

In the way that children have of being oddly untroubled by being sick itself, Joe was immediately more cheerful. Perhaps it had been one of those mysterious shortlived stomach upsets that are periodic hazards in the lives of small children. Perhaps it was a kind of involuntary act of empathy on this Good Friday. In my own visceral way, I understood how he felt. Whatever thrill the Meet had once had for me was gone.

As I had told Steve, I was still riding most Saturdays that winter and spring, meeting Mick in Dulwich village at 9.30 a.m. in all but the vilest weather. If it was raining when we woke up, each would leave it until about 8.30 a.m. before one called the other to confer or cancel.

He might cancel, but I would ride regardless. Unencumbered by children, Mick also lived only five minutes from the war memorial where we would meet. If it was wet, he could easily postpone his breakfast and go back to bed. In my case, I would have been up for a couple of hours at least, doing the early shift with the children (Ruth's lie-in being part of the exchange that gave me my ride). I would also have downed a large bowl of porridge. So by then, I did not care about the weather: to pass up my precious allotted hours of freedom would have been unthinkable.

From time to time I agonised over the deal. When I thought about it, my wish to go out for a ride sometimes struck me as unpardonably selfish. Ruth might check towards the end of the week whether I was planning a ride the next morning.

— Well, yes, I suppose so, I'd say . . . — But do you really think I should? It doesn't seem fair . . . to leave you with the kids all that time. Perhaps I shouldn't.

— Of course you should, she'd say, impatient only that I was once again asking permission. — You need your exercise. It's the only thing you do for *you*. It's probably a good outlet . . .

If I were going out with Mick, we rode side by side whenever the road allowed but we did not talk much. If we spoke, it was in

159

a reticent but easy shorthand – about work, our partners, what was taking place in our lives. Mostly, it felt like a necessary formality, to refer with a respectful lack of inquisitiveness to each other's hinterland. It was as though the rest of our lives was merely a side-show, the necessary backdrop which made possible the truly vivid experience of the here-and-now: turning the pedals, rolling along side-by-side, wheel matching wheel, in synch with our shared love of bike-riding.

When Mick's father became ill and died, I was still young enough that death had hardly touched my life. There had been a sixth-former at school who never returned after the summer holiday when his car was involved in a head-on collision. Years later, an old school friend of Ruth's was murdered while travelling in Thailand; I knew her too and shared the shock and sorrow. But the bizarre circumstances of her death, its utter randomness and sheer distance, made the loss difficult to assimilate. Though she was gone from our lives, her absence did not seem real. And we went on with our lives, like all young adults, assured of our own immortality.

After Mick's father died, I struggled to find the right words to express regret and sympathy, or to enable him to talk about his grief. Neither of us managed much beyond platitudes before drying up. It was no easier for Mick when Ruth fell ill.

He enquired. I provided an abbreviated medical bulletin.

After that, I would be happy to hit an incline and file out one behind the other. Then we would take turns to set the pace, listening to nothing but the rhythm of our own laboured breathing, calibrating no pain but the lactic in our legs.

They were companionable rides. I could still match him wheel for wheel most of the way, but we did not go as far afield as once we had. Three hours, or fifty miles, was our usual limit. Even then my stamina might start to flag on the way home, and I would have to let go his wheel on the final climb up Anerley Hill towards the Crystal Palace transmitter.

Once, at the top, I was cut up stupidly by a car on the roundabout. I chased after it down the Parade and, suddenly full of a rage that blew up from nowhere, bellowed something furious about his driving. The driver slowed and wound down the passenger-side window, shouting back, across his son in the front seat:

— What you going to do about it, you skinny cunt?

Skinny? *Skinny?* I weighed 80 kilos and had not thought of myself as skinny since I was a teenager. Of course, on a bike in black over-the-knee Lycra shorts, almost anyone looks skinny. But I was too nonplussed by the insult to manage more than a desultory *Wanker!* as he accelerated away. His son grinned back at me, pleased with the entertainment and proud of Dad.

Mick rode up.

— What was all that about? Mick asked when he caught up with me.

— Some bastard cut me up. Didn't like it when I yelled at him.

And that was an end to it. But I could tell that Mick, like me, was a little amazed by my righteous anger, how close to the surface it was and how violently it might erupt. In a sense I had been humiliated, yet I felt strangely powerful – in touch with some deep, if potentially dangerous resource I did not know I had.

There is a legend from the early days of the Tour de France, a time when there were no stages to the race, but one continuous epic of suffering and solidarity, pain and triumph. In those days, there were no service vehicles or team mechanics. If they punctured or fell, the riders were not even allowed to accept roadside assistance. They used to wear spare tubs around their shoulders, which made them look like guerrillas with bandoliers. Instead of today's tinted polycarbonate wraparounds, they wore aviator-style goggles to protect their eyes from the dust and grit of the unmade roads. After a wet day in the saddle, they would look like characters from the pages of Zola's *Germinal* – grime-stained coalminers rather than cyclists, the whites of their eyes shining with a harrowed luminosity from their streaked faces.

The story goes that the leading rider, ahead of his nearest rival by several hours, fell on a descent when the forks of his machine gave way. Doggedly, he picked himself up and carried the bicycle several miles to the next village. Once there, according to the rules of the race, he could take no outside help. So, when he had found a blacksmith's workshop, he set about repairing the broken fork himself. He lost his race lead the meanwhile, but eventually he succeeded in remounting and riding to the next relay. Only then did he learn of his disqualification – for accepting the assistance of a boy who had worked the bellows of the forge.

The man who founded the Tour de France, Henri Desgranges, was notorious among the riders for his planning of the toughest possible route and his equally harsh interpretation of the race's rules. A former professional rider himself, Desgranges earned the soubriquet *l'assassin* from those early tourists. It is the word they would mutter under their tortured breath as they saw his stolid figure impassively greet them at the summit of some blasted, lonely mountain pass. Cycle-racing is like that: it discovers the sadist, and the masochist, both within.

If it were wet and windy, and Mick had cancelled, I simply put on my Gore-Tex socks, shook out my rain-cape and set off, regardless, on a solo ride. The route I took might very well be the same – over my familiar North Downs, familiar even for the wet tarmac, slick with leaves, the sandy grit washed onto the road surface, and the raw wind which might be blustery and damp from the south-west or chill from the north-east. But the experience was subtly different.

Riding solo is an experience peculiar to itself, but all cyclists have something of the loner within. Even when you ride in a bunch, you ride first and foremost against yourself. You race against your own limitations.

Even in a group, cycling is scarcely a social activity. Often the only exchange for many miles might be a brief banal commentary on the state of the weather, the lumpiness of the road or the harshness of a gradient. Even when riding in a group at an easy tempo two-abreast, when conversation was unavoidable, the talk would mostly be of recent races and different circuits, of notable incidents like winning moves or bad crashes, who was riding strongly and who just followed wheels.

Riding solo always had a pleasant melancholy aspect for me. Some days I was happy to be alone with my thoughts, and for the sights and sounds and scents of those lanes to belong to me, in that moment, and to no other. At times, especially that year of Ruth's illness, the idea of talking to anyone, and being obliged to mediate the pure experience of riding, was irksome. Yet the fact of riding alone seemed to affirm my sense of loneliness and isolation, the inescapable privacy and particularity of what was happening in my life. Riding down those lanes, as they unfurled through the contours of the downland, the feeling was borne in on me that this, deserved or not, was my personal destiny and no one else's. I found myself coveting someone else's, anyone else's, life.

By the time I had turned for home, though, I always found

my mood lightened. Somehow, the familiarity of those roads, and the rhythm of pedal revolutions, and the measured stress of physical exercise, had eased something inside. Riding my bike exorcised the demon.

At some point, during Ruth's last year, I stopped shaving my legs.

Until then, I had kept up the old habit and tradition, if with less assiduous dedication. In the first year and a half of the children's lives, we would visit my parents almost monthly. I would help pack for those weekends – loading our hatchback with double-buggy, twin travel cots, bed linen and blankets, several changes of clothing for all parties concerned, and an industrial quantity of nappies. But I was already wearing my bib-shorts over a vest, and once the children were strapped into their child-seats, I would run in and pull on my favourite jersey – a replica of those worn by the Italian national squad, known as the *azzuri* after the team jersey's rich Mediterranean blue. In great haste, I would zip up the front, roll on the matching blue arm-warmers, don helmet and glasses, and roll out on my training bike, just as Ruth pulled away down our street.

I had worked out that the couple of hours it took to drive to my parents was – so far as the work of looking after the children was concerned – dead time. The wonder of automotive motion was that they could be guaranteed to sleep most of the way. So Ruth would drive, while I cycled. The countryside that filled the 55 miles between London and my parent's house in West Sussex was gently rolling, without any major hills. With a following wind and good legs, I could cover the distance in a shade over two and half hours. Depending on how delayed Ruth might be by traffic, my time by bike would be within an hour of hers in the car with the children. Ruth conceded the logic of the arrangement, and for me it was as close as I could get to a guilt-free morning of cycling.

I knew I was not fit enough to race any longer, but I had clung to the idea that I was still a racing cyclist. Recreational cyclists did not shave their legs; it was the mark of the serious bikie. I had not raced for more than a year; I had missed a whole season of training and racing. My legs were not so brown in the summer as once they had been, my torso not so whippet lean, but inside I secretly cherished the hope of a return to racing. I took a long-term view that my return might be as a veteran. I knew plenty of veterans, and I could wait. You need only be 40 to qualify as a veteran in cycling – it was less than a decade away. Forty did not seem so far off, I thought, provided I kept the faith and a modicum of fitness. The children would be nearly ten by then: off round friends' houses, out at martial arts or football practice, taking music lessons or doing ballet, and a thousand other things. Like cycling's old boys with their near-mystical belief in *muscle memory*, I reckoned I could pick up some form in a couple of months' serious training: I could be a pretty useful vet. In the meantime, I would be a sleeper. As long as I was shaving my legs, the flame of hope had still flickered.

Sometimes the peloton lets the lone escapist, the rider who slips the bunch, have his day. More often, though, there is too much at stake. The peloton regroups and starts to chase him down, mile by mile reeling him in. Once in their sights, they let him dangle out in front, the lone rider desperately maintaining a slim margin. They *hang him out to dry*. The strategy is quite impersonal: the logic is simply that as long as the escapist clings to his fragile advantage, there is no percentage for anyone else to launch an attack. The rider out in front strains every sinew to keep his precious seconds. For five minutes everyone knows his name, a glimpse of glory. In reality, he is doomed and there is a tragic inevitability about his fate. The peloton soon sweeps past, enveloping him once again in its multicoloured anonymity. Then he is forgotten, his brief heroic exploit subsumed by the larger collective drama of the race.

Like the bunch, implacable as a swarm of bees, life eventually overhauled me. The game was up. I had found I could not give up cycling, in the way that the phrase implies, with a single, irrevocable act of renunciation. I could only let it go, little by little, like paying out line to a kite which grows ever more distant, until finally the end of the twine slips through one's fingers, and the kite is away, gone on the wind. When it comes, it is an event that feels more like an accident than an exercise of will.

Our last holiday together was a week spent with Ruth's family on the Gower; a long, narrow peninsula whose patchwork of green fields and brown heath juts out west into the Atlantic from Swansea. The Gower bore a special significance for Ruth as a place familiar from family holidays of her childhood. Her father had taken them camping there. They would drive from Oxford to the Gower in a Mini, its roof-rack so overloaded with suitcases and camping gear that Ruth, as a child, would fear they'd be blown away as they crossed the mighty suspension bridge over the River Severn.

In those days, she liked to recall, a milkman used to deliver to tents in the dunes. The huge dunes themselves, extensive enough on a sunny day for another remake of *Beau Geste*, had been piled up at one end of the three-mile span of Rhossili Bay, so legend had it, by a single monstrous storm that had blasted the headland two hundred years earlier. One night, during one of these family holidays, a lesser though still impressive gale had blown their tent clean away. Her father had to lead his two daughters, half-blinded by the driving sand and rain, holding hands in convoy, until they reached the safety of a house of some friends up the road.

Ruth and I had also camped there, for a few days after our final exams, before the results came through. It rained on the first two days, which did little for our tense, irritable moods. Then, at last, the sun shone and we sunbathed nude in the dunes, so pleased to be warmed to the bone that we neglected to use enough suncream and both ended up badly sunburnt. We took turns driving back to Cardiff, where her parents lived, shaking and feverish.

This last holiday, in July, was, though none of us could quite think or believe it, a final family reunion. The children were just rising two. Lola was talking quite fluently, but Joe was still wrestling with words. He seemed frustrated by his inarticulacy. But none of us knew how to express what we all felt about his mother's gradually diminishing life.

I had brought my mountain bike, even on this of all holidays. I did not count on getting a ride; my old enthusiasm was new-tempered with realism. Yet it seemed inconceivable to be on holiday without taking a bicycle too.

Ruth's health was failing fast but I allowed myself not to see what was happening in front of my eyes. More than a month's treatment with strong steroids, prescribed prophylactically to reduce the *ædema* (the watery swelling) around the tumour in her brain, had slowly altered the shape of her face, rounding it out at the jowls in the drug's characteristic *goitre*. We were forced to learn these ugly new words that had invaded our lives. As the holiday went on, Ruth also complained frequently of headaches and began to have trouble sleeping. After a few days, she moved into a different bed in our holiday cottage, so that at night she would not be disturbed by me. Or disturb me, I didn't know which. She was profoundly depressed, hard to reach even if I had known how.

In the event, towards the end of the holiday, I did go out on my bike, while Ruth's mother helped babysit the children. Resolving to take no more than an hour, I headed up the hill through the village where wild ponies came to graze every morning. Then I struck out across the heath towards Rhossili Downs, the high saddle of land which lay like a sleeping giant along the back of the bay.

The morning was cool, the air moist. As I climbed, the breeze off the sea blew harder, damp with drizzle or, you could almost imagine, with spray from the surf crashing on the beach four hundred feet below. I rode to the headland at Rhossili itself, where the land forms a narrow green spit pointing straight out to sea until it collapses to a rocky causeway leading to the Worm's Head. When the tide is right, the swell causes a plume of spray to fire out of a blowhole close to the great outcrop's most westerly point – the snort of a slumbering Welsh dragon, we told the children.

Over that rough terrain, the five miles took nearly half an hour. Mindful of the clock, I turned round and started back. Only when I reached the highest point of the Downs, knowing I was less than ten minutes from home, did I stop to look at the view. I stood astride my bike, my eyes following the coastal path which skirted a little cluster of exposed rocks. Those boulders marked the highest point of an imposing cliff which forced the sea-breeze up over the Downs in a permanent near gale. I felt the wind sucking away the heat of my exertion, its roar drowning out even the sound of the waves over which it had so recently travelled in kinship. The sea stretched away, its cold metallic green ribbed with white-tops, until it disappeared into the horizon-less distance of drizzling grey cloud. With a little shiver, I turned for home.

Two months later Ruth died.

Stage 7

There had been a few times in Ruth's final days when, once the children were settled down for the night, I would ride over to the hospice where she was staying. By now it was the end of summer. Still preferring to wear shorts, not Lycra cycling shorts but ordinary cotton shorts, I would find the cooling September air chilly at first as I set out. I rode all the harder, churning my legs with unforgiving determination, until I arrived, perspiring, at the hospice gates. For a minute or two, I would feel I was intruding on its polite, compassionate hush with my laboured breathing.

There was little to do. I would bring her post, which now consisted almost entirely of cards from friends and well-wishers. I might read them quickly to her if she were too tired or detached to do so herself, as was often now the case. I would ask how she was feeling, whether she needed anything. I would sit holding her hand and say a few words about how the children had been that day if she had not seen them. After a while, I would kiss her goodnight and leave. I did not know what else to do.

When I left, it would be cooler still. But the freshness now made me want to fill my lungs greedily with the night air. I would ride fast again, to warm myself up. I would ride as fast as I could, charging through gaps, overtaking cars on the inside, slipstreaming buses at full speed, sprinting through lights as they turned red, fuelled by rage and desperation. Until a sobering thought brought me up short: what if something happened to me? what then for the children? I could not afford such risk-taking. And I could not afford to feel that I did not deserve to live.

While Ruth was alive and well, I could still entertain a fantasy of evasion and escape. I went on shaving my legs. I would daydream at work about the coming weekend's ride. My personal highlights, those peak moments from a racing life, remained crisp and vivid in my mind's eye. The dream of racing once again, at some unspecified future date, I kept alive like an illicit affair. A secret longing that was my taste of infidelity.

After Ruth's death, the dream also slowly died. I knew that being left on my own with two small children meant one inescapable fact: the only role that mattered now was to be as good a parent as I could. It goes without saying that I underestimated the extent of this challenge many times over, but I was accurate in one respect: my life as a serious bikie was over. Weekends and evenings had to be family time. Any hours that I wasn't working, there was enough to do on my own just with the household chores of cooking, cleaning, shopping and laundry; the children had to make do with little enough of my time and attention as it was. The way in which the demands of family life finally defeat solitary male pursuits is completely commonplace. It happens all the time; it is a cliché even. But for most, it takes place gradually, over time, so that there is a staged withdrawal, a process of adjustment. The only difference between me and other men, I believed, was that for me there was no shading, none of the fuzzy ambiguity of life slowly evolving from one thing into another. Everything had the clarity and definition of being stated in absolutes. That was your life then; this is your life now.

So I thought. And yet, a paradox developed. For many months after Ruth's death, I was offered so much help by both the children's grandmothers that on almost every other weekend I had the time and encouragement to give myself a break and go for a ride. What was true for me, that I needed the children to pull me through the worst of times, was true for Ruth's mother especially. The children were our saving grace. They gave the grieving adults solace by providing a sense of purpose and the need to maintain a continuity in life. Sharing parenting with someone other than one's partner, however, was not always easy.

— No, no more biscuits. Daddy says you've had enough already . . . Oh, all right, all right: just one more then. But after that, no more, because Daddy says so.

The contours of the relationships might be familiar, but Ruth's loss – her absence as mother, as daughter, as wife – raised the stakes immeasurably. It made everything matter, gave an emotional weight to every little word and deed. Rather than try clumsily to assert my authority as parent, which usually only made me irritable and disqualified me further in the attempt, it seemed better to absent myself for a few hours. And so the strange situation developed where I rode my bike more than I had for several months during the last stages of Ruth's illness.

If I felt guilty about this, I recalled what Ruth had said. *You need your exercise. It's the only thing you do for* you. *It's probably a good outlet* . . . If my cycling embodied a loyalty to the way things once used to be, it also seemed a kind of loyalty to her. In any case, to carry on as much as possible in the old way, just to press numbly on, seemed the safest course.

Those rides, usually solo, did take on a different aspect. I no longer treated them as training for some future return to my racing career. I cycled more within myself. I would still ride the hills, but at a more gentle tempo. I did not want to hurt myself for some abstract ideal of fitness. I preferred instead to take in the views, to smell the air. Physical existence now appeared a relatively fragile fact, not to be relied upon; I would not abuse it by treating my body like an engine, a machine made only to be driven hard.

I would remember, with a shudder, the times I had crashed in races. The time when the break of four I was in had overcooked it on a blind corner. Three of us had fallen. As my bike left the road, I somersaulted over a little grassy traffic island and crash-landed on the tarmac on the far side, skidding feet-first into the hedge. When I stopped cursing and hopping up and down with the pain, I went to pick up my bent bike. When I saw the path I had taken, airborne, I realised I had missed by inches a stout steel post which bore the road-sign marking the bend. Only now, in retrospect, did that near-miss become a chastening moment.

No longer would I tuck into a crouch on a long descent and force myself not to touch the brakes even on a tightening curve. The point of pure speed somehow now escaped me. Instead of fantasies of riding far and free, conquering alpine mountain passes and flying back to earth through scores of hairpins, my imagination would be cluttered with scenarios of possible accidents. The old aggression, the desire to push myself and find new limits, was gone. In place of the raw joy of riding fast and reckless, I found myself preoccupied with constant mental calculations of risk. The thrill was gone.

As long as I was riding more, I saw more of Mick. Nothing was said between us, but we were conscious of how much our friendship was nourished by and depended on the time spent in each other's company in the saddle. Cycling had a different emphasis in each of our lives. While it was a central feature, as I thought, of my identity, cycling remained something separate and contained, parcelled off from the rest of my life; and so there had always been a barrier to integrating the people I knew through cycling. For Mick, there was no conflict; it was all continuity. He worked in a bike shop. He rode his bike to work. He rode it home afterwards. He lived close to the Herne Hill stadium; during the season, he trained or raced there every week. In a literal sense, his life revolved around cycling. I sometimes envied the way his life seemed all of a piece, without the contradictions I felt.

Mick could see the difficulty I had, now more than ever, in reconciling the demands life made on me. He was sympathetic, and as a way of integrating cycling into my life a little more, he encouraged me to participate in the cyclo-cross races he rode over the winter. These races were quick and easy to reach – often they took place no further afield than the suburban parks of outer London. And because they lasted little more than an hour, cross-races would make fewer demands of my limited fitness. At the top echelon, cross-races are as competitive and hard-fought as any species of competitive cycling, but at the entry level they are the nearest thing cycle-racing permits to a fun ride.

Cross-races are a traditional form of winter racing, a species of off-road racing that existed long before mountain bikes arrived to make dirt-track riding a popular pastime. Cross-bikes looked much like racing bikes, except for being fitted with higher gearing, fatter tyres, beefed-up brakes and larger clearances between frame and wheels so that they did not become clogged by mud. Serious cross-racers would often have two machines, swapping between them every lap or so in really muddy conditions while a helper would hose or scrub the dirt off in the interval. As a soggy cross course became churned up after successive circuits, a bike might quickly pick up several pounds of extra ballast in the form of glutinous brown mud. When you reached one of the sections where you had to shoulder the bike and carry it, then you'd notice the extra weight as the top tube bounced painfully on your shoulder. Cyclo-cross's administrators had been smart enough to deregulate the sport to permit riders to use mountain bikes in their races. Serious cross-riders still used cross-bikes on the faster courses, but on the more technical circuits the whole field would be on MTBs.

One chill and misty Sunday a little over a year after Ruth's death, I packed my gear in the back of the car, my children and mother-in-law in the front, and drove down to a waterlogged piece of farmland on the Surrey–Sussex border. Around we went, on a mile circuit between thickets, across ditches, along tracks and through drowning pasture-land. For the first time in my life, my own children were spectating and supporting. Every lap of ten, as I came past the finish, every lap more covered in the melted chocolate mud, there they were. Waving and shouting, 'Come on, Daddy, you're winning, you're winning.' I smiled and waved back as I passed. Feeling myself their hero spurred me on, and I rode above myself. Although Mick was much fitter, I finished ahead of him after his bike got stuck in one gear. I was still placed well down the field. I didn't stop to find out exactly where.

I queued to use the hose to spray the mud off my machine. The children had to wait while I cleaned myself up and changed out of the back of the car. Finally we left. Though the children had eaten nothing but a couple of bananas between them, and had missed lunch, they soon fell fast asleep on the drive home on roads now mired with Sunday afternoon traffic. It was a day's outing for an hour's ride, I realised – and all to service my old compulsion.

As the euphoria of the event and the quick-hit exercise high faded, a pall of guilt about what I had just inflicted on my children and their grandmother settled over me. What *really* could be more dreary than bystanding in a freezing sodden field for an hour, while I covered myself not in glory but in slurry, and then hanging around for another hour afterwards, while I washed the field's residue off myself and my bike? What could any of it possibly mean to them?

But cycling does nothing if not make one single-minded and dogged (or perhaps the doggedness and monomania are already there embryonically within those that choose cycling). I drew no conclusions from that day in the mud. I kept on taking the opportunities that were offered to get a ride. Working steadily through my relatives and their goodwill, I took my mother along to mind the children while I took part in a race round a park near Blackheath, in London's south-east corner. A part of me was thrilled that I still had the legs to compete. I was far off the pace of the front-runners, but I could hold my own and ride my own race. The recreational rides I would do when I visited my parents, taking my mountain bike up and down the bridlepaths of the South Downs which started barely a mile from their house, had given me some experience of the technicalities of off-road cycling – negotiating tree-roots, steep inclines, rutted descents. It felt good to be wearing those knee-length thermal shorts, competition jersey, track-mitts, Gore-Tex socks and cleated shoes – all that Lycra-knit figure-hugging garb – for some real purpose.

Where once, the purist, I had disdained mountain biking as not proper cycling, now I embraced it. It had time-efficiency on its side: an off-road ride of a little more than an hour's duration felt the equivalent workout of a road-based ride of more than twice that time. There was virtually no freewheeling when you were riding off-road. To stay up upright, you had to keep pushing the pedals and keep turning those fat, knobbly tyres through the dirt. I did not have speed or stamina, but the off-road riding that I was doing meant that I kept a reasonable level of aerobic fitness. Even if I had had the time to commit to it, which I did not, road-racing demanded a level of form merely to take part that I knew I no longer had.

Mountain biking was a way of keeping my cycling, prolonging its life, for as long as I could. Looked at another way, with hindsight perhaps, it was part of a long, slow staged withdrawal. It was my methadone programme. At the time, it appeared simply as the compromise between the old habits and the new circumstances which then seemed workable and sustainable. There is our loyalty to present living things – the attachment to what we know, the tug of obligation to others, the pleasure of obeying conditioned behaviour – but what is so easy to underestimate in life is the loyalty we have to the past and passing things, the dead and the dying. Letting go is harder than holding on.

The year had turned, and I had not ridden for two or three weeks, when Mick invited me to join him in a cross-race up at

Eastway. Eastway had a certain appeal. Less than half-an-hour away, it was (besides Herne Hill) easily the most accessible place to race from central London. And for all its ugly bleakness, I had a certain affection for it as the venue for the beginning of my competitive cycling: the road circuit was where I had raced my first time-trials a decade earlier, and won the first point on my licence. I had never ridden the off-road circuit that was incorporated into the landscaped gullies and hummocks that filled the space bounded by the tarmac loop, but I blithely agreed to take part. With the shelter afforded by its clubhouse, I considered it would be a good place to take the children along with my then new girlfriend, Anna, who had never seen me race and for whom, I felt, the idea of cycle-racing seemed at least a little exotic, even romantic.

By the time the day race came round, I wondered at the wisdom of it. The misgivings had started piling up. Several weeks had passed since I had ridden a bike in anger. I worried that what little semblance of fitness I had had earlier that winter would have ebbed away. The prospect of Eastway itself, on a cold, grey January day, seemed to me an entirely forbidding prospect for my little group of involuntary spectators. I was conscious, too, of requiring Anna, whom I had only met two months earlier, to fulfil the babysitting function previously filled by one or other grandmother. From whatever angle I looked, it did not seem auspicious. Against all this, which left me with little enough appetite for the race, I had promised Mick I would be there and felt I could not let him down.

The off-road circuit was longer than most and faster. It suited the true cross-rider much more than the weekend mountain-bikie like me. The field was far more competitive, including the national cross champion and a score of aspirants. Besides Mick, I did not recognise a single other rider. A whole generation of tough, young bikies seemed to have come up in the years since I'd last raced in earnest. I felt, at the age of thirty-three, like an old-timer – and a raw novice all over again. In the changing rooms the atmosphere was brusque and businesslike; there was none of the banter and comradeship I had enjoyed in the shabby, tin-roofed village halls across south-east England.

Within seconds of the start, I became a backmarker. I pushed myself hard but, in this company, I was woefully slow. Within half a dozen circuits, I was lapped by the front-runners. A tall, lean teenager wearing a national champion's jersey and riding a white cross-bike went past me as smooth and strong as if he were riding on the road not a dirt-track. A few minutes later, the first small chasing group tore furiously past me. There are few things, in cycling, so demoralising as being lapped. I pressed on, aiming at least to finish, but, on that long, drab, exposed circuit, the full futility of the exercise was now borne in upon me. Given my preparation for the race, this was only to be expected, but everyone has their pride. There had been a time, I reflected bitterly, when I would not have been so easily humiliated.

After the first lap Anna had used my camera to take some snaps as I came round. Now, though, the harsh January blast across Hackney Marsh had driven her and the children into the low clubhouse. There was no one cheering for me as I passed; but there was little to cheer for. Nearing the end of the eighth lap, my strength was failing. I came to the foot of a steep bank where riders were forced to dismount and carry. I almost fell off my bike, and stood for a second, sweating, pale and trembling, unsure whether I could summon the energy to hoist my bike on my shoulder and clamber up the slope. In a technical sense, I had *blown up*, as cyclists say. My body had used all its available stores of glycogen; my legs were clogged with lactic acid. There was nothing left in the tank. Confused and nauseated, I paused for a second and thought about whether to struggle on. Then I realised, not exactly that I could not do it, but that I did not have to.

There had been a time when the shame of *packing* had spurred me on, to finish no matter what. That pride had driven me to be fitter so that I could keep pace and stay the course. But now the will was gone; my heart was no longer in it. I pushed my bike back to the clubhouse. In due course, someone would enter the letters DNF – Did Not Finish – next to my name on the start sheet, but my part in the race might never merit even that record. I showered, packed up my bike, gathered up my family, and left. It was over.

— Are you OK? Anna asked in the car, still a little worried by my glassy-eyed appearance when I had first got back to the clubhouse.

— Yes, I'm better . . . I'm sorry: I shouldn't have dragged you all up here. It was pointless.

— No, it wasn't. You wanted to race. I was happy to watch you with the children.

— Well, there wasn't much to watch. I don't want to race again. That's it; I'm finished with it.

— You can race if you want, she says. — But I wish you wouldn't push yourself so hard.

— You don't understand. You can't do it by half-measures. It's pointless racing if you're just going to ride around. You have to be fit and you have to train, and I can't make that sort of commitment.

— Did you win, Daddy? asked Joe, from the back seat. He

can't stand hearing a conversation between us for more than a few seconds without wanting to be involved.

— No, I didn't win. I didn't even finish the race.

I felt I should somehow soften this news for him, that I should acquiesce with his automatic belief in his father's all-conquering heroism. But I was too depressed.

— Did you crash? interjected Lola, always looking for the rational explanation.

— No, I was just too tired, and I was right at the back. So I had to get off and give up.

A morose silence, matching my mood, settled inside the car. As though I had not already made extravagant and unreasonable demands of their loyalties to me by dragging them all to this gloomy stretch of East London, I felt even more of an ogre for spurning one by one the sympathy and support each in turn offered me.

They don't deserve this, I thought, as we passed back beneath Tower Bridge and towards home. Never again.

All my journeys by bike seemed, at the outset, to offer the promise of liberty and discovery and each venturing-out suggested new possibility and choice. The unfettered freedom of the road was the lure of every ride. But it seems to me now that almost the opposite was true, that those rides were always about return. As though I were attached by an invisible thread of elastic which stretched, then contracted, reeling me in towards home. What began with limitless options became a narrowing number of available routes, until I found myself once again back at my own front door. Almost without knowing how I had arrived there, as if hypnotised by the turning pedals and spinning wheels, automatically piloted down lanes and streets so familiar that every foot of tarmac was known, every gradient mentally tabulated for the effort required, every perspective etched in the memory, I had come full circle.

First, I wish to salute the cyclists of South London, especially those members of my club, the Vélo Club de Londres, and, besides, those members of the Dulwich Paragon, De Laune, Sydenham Wheelers, Catford, Dartford and West Kent cycling clubs, with whom it was once my privilege to ride and race.

Among my own unofficial league of wheelmen, I owe particular debts to: Tommy Barlowe, Phil Burnett, Dave Creasey, Alex Jones, Martin Lydon, Sean McKibben, Bob Ruskowski, Don Wiley, Russell Williams. Behind them are legions of others, too numerous to mention, who deserve either my specific thanks or general gratitude for what they have contributed to a great amateur sport which, like all amateur sports, survives only by the enthusiasm and selflessness of those who are part of it. In this book, some names have been changed out of respect for the privacy of individuals concerned.

On the writing side, my thanks are due to David Godwin and Nicholas Pearson, in both cases for their enthusiasm, support, patience and editorial intelligence. A special mention is due also to Alison Truefitt, an expert copyeditor and a writer's dream reader.

Finally, I would like to thank my immediate family: my parents, Geoff and Caroline, and brother, Tom; my late wife, Ruth Picardie; my son, Joe, and daughter, Lola; and my wife, Anna Shapiro. Without them, nothing would have been written.

PERMISSIONS

William Saroyan, *The Bicycle Rider in Beverly Hills* Ballantine New York (1971)

Mark Twain: from an essay 'Taming the Bicycle'. This article was published in *Wheelmen*, vol. 3, no. 1, Winter (1972)

W H Auden 'Miss Gee' in Selected Poems (ed) E. Mendelson, Faber & Faber, (1979)

R. N. Khurana: from 'Bicycle: A Teacher of Human Values'. This article was published in *Indian Bicycle Ambassador*, June (1990)

Adam Philips, *Houdini's Box: On the Arts of Escape*. Faber & Faber (2001)